TEXT BY
LAWRENCE E. BABITS

Published by Eastern National, copyright 2002.

Eastern National provides quality educational products and services to
America's national parks and other public trusts.

Thanks to Diane Depew, Linda Brown, Ann Childress, Rick Hatcher, Don Long, Chris Revels,
Pat Ruff, Farrell Saunders and Eric Williams of the National Park Service.

Front cover: *The Battle of Cowpens* by Don Troiani,
courtesy of Historical Art Prints, Ltd., Southbury, CT.

Back cover: *The Surrender of Cornwallis at Yorktown*, by John Trumbull,
courtesy of The U.S. Capitol Historical Society.

Printed on recycled paper.

To order additional titles in this series or other national park-related items,
please call 1-800-821-2903, or visit our online store at www.eParks.com.

# SOUTHERN CAMPAIGNS OF THE AMERICAN REVOLUTION

When Lexington and Concord, Massachusetts, militiamen fired at British troops on April 19, 1775, the revolt spread rapidly throughout the colonies. In the South, how one chose sides depended on many factors including promises for advancement, command and wealth, previous alliances and feuds, and how one's neighbors saw the struggle.

During the Revolutionary War, several southern military episodes had a pronounced impact on the ultimate American victory. In the first months of fighting, Virginia, North Carolina and South Carolina Patriots consolidated their hold and drove opponents into exile or thoroughly cowed them. At Charles Town (Charleston), South Carolina, rebels repulsed a British assault on the city. The victories gave the South a two-year grace period to organize several state governments and put together an effective military force.

A second British effort to subdue the southern colonies fell on the Patriots with devastating results in December 1778. After Savannah, Georgia, was taken, British forces moved rapidly up the Savannah River, and by mid-spring 1779, Georgia was, nominally, once again a royal colony.

The next year, a reinforced British army took Charles Town in May 1780. This defeat wiped out the southern Continental Army as virtually all Continentals from Georgia, the Carolinas and Virginia were taken prisoner. Again, the British moved rapidly inland and reestablished royal control throughout most of the state behind a screen of outposts. When a new American army came to South Carolina that summer, it was defeated at Camden.

Unfortunately for the planned British pacification, some Loyalist militia began taking revenge for earlier treatment by

A 1776 VIEW OF CHARLES TOWN, THE CAPITAL OF SOUTH CAROLINA

(LC)

Patriots. When Tories (Loyalists) raided paroled Americans' farms, opposition crystallized almost immediately and the Patriots grew in strength and boldness. Many skirmishes took place between Loyalists and Patriots in the Carolina back-country, but after the British defeat at Musgrove's Mill in August 1780, Loyalists won no significant victory in this vicious partisan warfare.

While the main British force moved north and occupied Charlotte, North Carolina, other detachments attempted to subjugate the rebellious backcountry. At Kings Mountain, Patriot overmountain men wiped out a Loyalist force under Major Patrick Ferguson. This defeat destroyed the unit protecting the British army's flank and forced Lieutenant General Earl Charles Cornwallis to temporarily withdraw from North Carolina.

By December 1780, American hopes in the South were glum indeed. When a Rhode Islander, Major General Nathanael Greene, General George Washington's handpicked commander to save the South, arrived in Charlotte, he found a battered, starving army and a civilian smallpox epidemic. Despite the gloomy outlook, Greene, ten months later, had defeated the British and made a major contribution to the Patriot cause.

Greene divided his forces, threatening widely separated British garrisons. British reactions led to the Patriot victory at Cowpens (January 17, 1781). Although Greene was forced out of the Carolinas, Cornwallis ruined his own army in the pursuit, and Greene quickly returned to North Carolina. After the battle at Guilford Courthouse (March 15, 1781), the British moved to the coast to obtain supplies, then marched to join British forces in Virginia.

MAJOR GENERAL
NATHANAEL GREENE

(NA)

The stage was set for the campaign resulting in the British surrender at Yorktown, Virginia (October 19, 1781).

While Cornwallis invaded Virginia, Greene redeemed the South. Greene's "war of posts" was successful, even as larger, main force engagements were tactically successful for crown forces. The British "victories" at Hobkirk's Hill (April 25, 1781) and Ninety Six (May-June 1781) were hollow because Camden was evacuated and Ninety Six was abandoned. As summer turned to fall, Greene fought the British to a standstill at Eutaw Springs in September. By November 1781, British forces were confined to the coastal zone between Charles Town and Savannah where they could neither feed themselves nor generate Loyalist support.

Coupled with the American-French victory at Yorktown, Virginia, the war was winding down but it would be another

# Glossary

**Backcountry** — The southern interior adjacent to the frontier. This was a thinly settled zone of small farms and few towns.

**Battalion** — See Regiment.

**Bayonet** — A long, pointed blade that could be mounted on the end of a musket. The bayonet allowed men to attack and defend themselves when their musket was unloaded. In 18th-century tactics, the bayonet charge was frequently used by both British and American regulars.

A PATRIOT OF 1776 DEFENDING HIS HOMESTEAD.

(LC)

**Company** — In 18th-century military organizations, a company was a smaller unit within a battalion. It was usually commanded by a captain and at full strength numbered 100 men.

**Continental** — The American regulars. These men were enlisted for three years or "during the war." Most were well trained and fully the equal of British regulars on southern battlefields. Late in the war, due to a shortage of enlistments, some Continentals were enlisted for only eighteen months. The Continental Army was a standing or permanent army during the war.

**Crown** — See Royalist.

**Dragoon** — A cavalryman.

**Flank** — The end of a line, left and right.

**Forlorn Hope** — The leading element of an assault party. They were called this because few had much chance of surviving.

**Light Infantry** — Lightly equipped, highly mobile troops.

**Loyalist** — See Tory

**Militia** — Initially, the colonial self-defense force. During the Revolution, militia were placed in classes called up for local service as needed. Generally, they served for short periods, such as six weeks or three months. In emergencies, they might be called out for only a few days. Generally, the militia were not well trained and they did not turn out in great numbers or in a timely fashion. They usually only fought in their own state or a nearby state.

**Musket** — The most common shoulder arm of the Revolutionary War. This was a smoothbore

year before British troops left the South. The southern campaigns had been an opportunity for the British to retain some American colonies but they resulted in the British losing the war.

In this booklet, the southern campaigns are divided into an introductory overview, the early war events, the Savannah - Charles Town - Camden Campaigns when the British regained control over parts of the

SHOWN LEFT TO RIGHT: SOUTH CAROLINA MILITIAMAN, 1780; LEE'S LEGION LT. INFANTRY PRIVATE; BRITISH GRENADIER, 33RD REGIMENT; 3RD CONTINENTAL LIGHT DRAGOON

weapon to which one could attach a bayonet. The musket was easier and faster to load than a rifle but its accurate range was only about 50 yards.

**Parole, paroled** — A prisoner's word of honor on being released that he will not bear arms until exchanged. Once "on parole," a man was supposed to remain neutral until exchanged for a prisoner from the other side. People on parole were not to be harassed; if they were, the parole was considered to be violated, releasing them from their neutrality.

**Partisan, partizan** — A volunteer soldier, not an enlisted Continental or militiaman, who fought with a raiding style of warfare. The modern term is guerrilla.

**Patriot** — A person who served his country. Since the Whigs won and the American colonies became independent, the term has come to mean one who supported the Whig side in the Revolutionary War. In reality, both Whig and Tory saw their actions as patriotic.

**Pioneer** — In 18th-century military terminology, a pioneer was a soldier responsible for building fortifications, repairing roads, and general construction.

**Provincial** — An American Tory who served in a colonial military unit on the British side on a full-time basis. This term was also used to identify these colonial units in the British army. The Volunteers of Ireland serving under Rawdon were a provincial unit.

**Redoubt** — A small, earthen fort without bastions placed in a critical defensive area.

**Regiment** — A military formation composed of at least four, and as many as ten companies. A lieutenant colonel or colonel commanded a regiment. Regiment and battalion were often used interchangeably during the Revolutionary War.

**Regular** — A British soldier. These men were enlisted for long service and were generally well-trained and disciplined.

**Rifle** — A specialized form of musket (or small arm) that had grooves cut into the inside of its barrel. These grooves caused the bullet to spin, giving greater accuracy. Rifles were slower to load and one could not attach a bayonet. Rifles were generally used by specialized units or frontiersmen who had considerable practice in their use.

**Royal, royalist** — Pertaining to and supporting the king, or king's side, during the American Revolution.

**State Troops** — Some American states raised their own "regulars," who were not supposed to serve outside the state border. These men generally enlisted for 18 months, or half the term demanded of Continentals.

**Tidewater** — This term refers to the coastal zone in the southern states. In many cases, it actually extended further inland than the precise area affected by the tide.

**Tory** — An American supporter of the king. The opposite of a Whig.

**Whig** — An American who supported the revolutionary movement against royal authority.

South, the partisan war as the rebellion heated up again, thwarting the British with victories at Kings Mountain and Cowpens, redeeming the South and the campaign in Virginia. These are not distinctions made during the war but they have a certain utility for organizing a diverse series of battles, campaigns and operations for a better understanding of the Revolutionary War in the South.

## THE EARLY WAR YEARS — 1775-1778

The war's first months were essentially a holding action in the South. Virginia and the Carolinas disposed of those who rallied to the Crown in a series of small but important skirmishes. In Charles Town, Patriot defenders repulsed a major British seaborne assault.

In the Carolina backcountry, Tory and Patriot alignments were difficult to predict in 1775-76 and may reflect earlier feuding between groups migrating from further north. Complicating matters still further, the constant threat of Indian raids caused both factions to cooperate on occasion. Once Loyalists were known to be encouraging raids, many lukewarm supporters joined in common opposition to the Indians.

The first southern encounter between Patriot and Tory took place in the South Carolina backcountry at Ninety Six. The Loyalists, or "Scovelites," as they were called by the Patriots, seized a munitions convoy on November 3, 1775. Both sides then gathered their forces and Tories under Patrick Cunningham attacked Patriots at Ninety Six. After a brief three-day siege, a truce was called to allow the leaders to settle differences. Despite the truce, South Carolina sent more troops and asked North Carolina for help. Under the command of Colonel William Richardson, a mixed group of militia and Continentals numbering over a thousand men forced the Tories into the Cherokee Country. After several skirmishes during the "Snow Campaign," Tory leaders were captured and the frontier rested a little easier although the constant threat of Indian war still hung over the frontier.

The Tories dealt with, backcountry militia went after the Indians. The biggest threat came from Cherokees who, in March 1775, without advising Crown officials, sold some of their land to settlers already in residence in the Holston, Nolichucky and Watauga River valleys. In May 1776, a Great Council of the Cherokees, pressured by British agents, ordered "overmountain"

frontiersmen off their land within
twenty days.

Settlers ignored the eviction order
and, by July, outraged Cherokees began
raiding, striking the Carolina backcountry
and overmountain settlements. The
response was rapid. North Carolina's
Griffith Rutherford joined Andrew
Williamson west of the Blue Ridge
Mountains, leading over 4,000 men into the
Cherokee homeland. Militia burned villages
and destroyed crops during September.
Virginians arrived in October and devastat-
ed the Overhill Cherokee towns. The
Cherokee were effectively driven out of
the war and a widespread perception of
Tory involvement caused many settlers to
actively support the Patriots.

During the fall of 1775, another serious threat occurred in coastal Virginia.
After Patriot threats caused Loyalist
Governor Dunmore to take refuge on a
British warship, he commenced raiding
York River plantations. Even more disturbing to Virginians was word that Dunmore
was arming slaves, offering freedom for
enlistment in the Royal Regiment of
Ethiopians. By November, the regiment
had some 300 armed men. With "Liberty to
Slaves" printed across their uniform frocks,
they were ready to fight.

Virginia and North Carolina troops
marched against the British force that
included some regulars in addition to the
Royal Ethiopians. At Great Bridge outside
Norfolk, Virginia, the Patriots routed
Dunmore and his supporters but could do
little about the small fleet he controlled.
On New Year's Day 1776, Dunmore bombarded Norfolk, then sent landing parties
to burn the town. The Patriots, not sympa-
thetic to Norfolk which they considered "a
nest of Tories," followed up the British raid

by burning almost all remaining houses.
Dunmore finally sailed away from the
Chesapeake Bay and, it was later reported,
sold most of his African soldiers back into
slavery in the West Indian cane fields.
This minor engagement largely freed
Virginia from most British interference
until late 1780.

A North Carolina engagement with
similar results occurred at Moores Creek
Bridge on February 27, 1776. Loyalist
militia, chiefly Scottish Highlanders and
ex-Regulators, marched toward the coast

because they had been promised British arms, supplies and support at Wilmington. Following the leadership of 60-year-old Colonel Donald McDonald, a veteran of the Scottish uprising that ended at Culloden in April 1746, over 1,500 Tories began marching from Cross Creek near present-day Fayetteville, North Carolina. After two weeks of maneuvering, the Loyalists tried to force their way over Moores Creek in present-day Pender County, North Carolina.

The attack was difficult because swamps restricted mobility, over half the Tories were without guns, and the little bridge had been stripped of planking, limiting access to the opposite shore. On the American side of the stream, 900 Patriots under Alexander Lillington and Richard Caswell waited behind a breastwork with two cannon.

Following Donald McLeod, a younger, more impulsive officer, and Captain John Campbell, the vanguard, carrying broadswords rushed onto the bridge timbers. Shouting Gaelic war cries and,

"King George and Broadswords," the forlorn hope tried to force their way across. The skirmish was over in minutes, but pursuit lasted for several days as successful Patriots apprehended and disarmed every Loyalist they could. Only two Patriots were wounded, one mortally; the Tories lost at least thirty killed and over 800 captured. Had the piedmont Tories reached Wilmington and joined coastal Loyalists, defeating them might not have been so easy. If promised British support arrived, North Carolina might have had serious problems establishing any Patriot control. The aborted rising set the tone for other attempts by North Carolina Tories. Virtually every time they rose, often against specific instructions to wait, Patriots defeated them before the British army arrived.

In late June, Charles Town successfully resisted a British raid by holding Fort Sullivan against naval bombardment and land assault by British regulars. Charles Town's defensive preparations began late in 1775 but not much was accomplished before the British fleet arrived off the bar

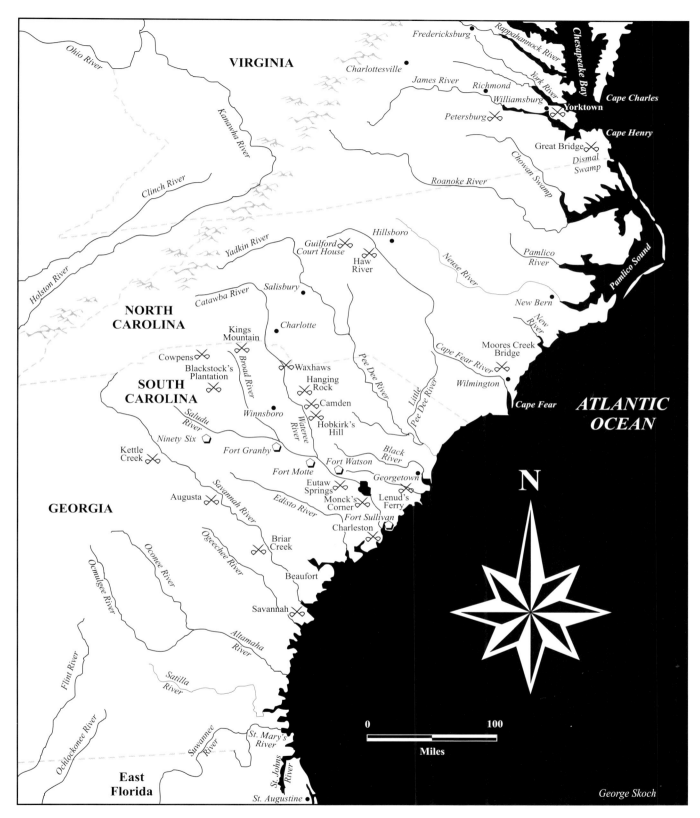

THE SOUTHERN CAMPAIGN OF THE AMERICAN REVOLUTION
*Key towns, battles and geographical locations of the Southern Theater of Operations, 1775–1783.*

at the end of May 1776. By June 4, when General Charles Lee arrived to take command, perhaps as many as fifty ships,

men-of-war and transports, were blockading the harbor. The main point of resistance was a palmetto log fortification on Sullivan's Island. When finally attacked on June 28, the fort was only half finished but it was ready enough.

Sir Peter Parker's warships anchored 400 yards off the fort and opened fire on Colonel William Moultrie's garrison. The sand and log fortification absorbed the

British shot with little damage. The nine warships were not so lucky. American fire directed by Major Francis Marion punished the fleet mercilessly. Three ships ran aground and when the *Acteon* could not get off, it was doomed. Unable to move, it was battered by Fort Sullivan and finally set afire by her crew.

In conjunction with the naval bombardment, infantry attempted to hit Fort Sullivan from the rear. Fortunately for the Patriots defending Sullivan's Island, the tide came in and the effort was thwarted. British casualties were heavy, perhaps as many as 200 were killed or wounded, including the mortally wounded captains of *Bristol* and *Experiment*. Parker himself suffered minor splinter wounds. The Americans lost about ten killed and two dozen wounded, in large part because the soft palmetto logs did not splinter when struck by cannon fire. A hero emerged in Sergeant William Jasper, who jumped into the fort ditch to retrieve the colors when they were shot away.

Once overt resistance was done away with, the new southern states protected

their frontiers and dealt with raiding parties. On three occasions, expeditions moved against the British base at St. Augustine, Florida, but these optimistic efforts never passed Georgia's Altamaha River. In response, Florida-based Loyalist refugees raided Georgia and South Carolina on an intermittent, but bloody basis. The raids accomplished little except to infuriate both sides, raising animosity to levels that encouraged repeated atrocities as the war progressed.

## THE BRITISH REGAIN CONTROL: THE MID-YEARS — 1778-1780

After two years of relative peace, war returned to the South in December 1778. The long delay allowed local governments to establish control over their territory but did not eliminate long standing local animosity which often had little to do with the rebellion. Frustrated by their inability to destroy Washington's army or achieve concrete results in the North, the British turned south. Encouraged by refugee reports of strong Loyalist support in Georgia and the Carolinas, home country instructions authorized retaking southern states. Initial efforts proved promising, even though their assumptions about local support were incorrect.

Under Archibald Campbell, 3,500 soldiers were sent to St. Augustine to join British troops already there. Once at sea, Campbell exploited vague instructions and attacked Savannah on December 29, 1778. The outnumbered American defenders were changing commanders and were hindered by a lack of cooperation between Continentals and militia. The attack was an

Savannah Fort, with 8 pieces of Cannon, seemed to cover the Left Flank of the Rebel Line; and the Town of Savannah, round which there was an old Entrenchment, lay in their Rear ... I determined that the Light Infantry should make an Impression upon the Enemy's Right, while I should in person attack the Rebel Line in Front ... Our Cannon ... broke the Enemy's Line before we had reached the marshy Rivulet, which the Highlanders crossed with an Alacrity peculiar to themselves. But although not a Moment was to be lost in advancing upon the Rebels, it was scarcely possible to come up with them: Their Retreat was rapid beyond Conception. ... the greatest part of the Rebel Brigades [, cut off] from the Augusta Road, ... hurried ... towards Yamacraw, in the hope of making their Escape through the Swamps on that side of the Town. ... Unfortunately ... it was Flood Tide; and such only who could swim effected their Escape. — Archibald Campbell, Lieutenant Colonel, 71st Regiment

*Journal of An Expedition against the Rebels of Georgia in North America*, Richmond County Historical Society, Ashantilly Press, Darien, Georgia; 1981.

American disaster because Campbell was both able and aggressive.

American defenses were quickly penetrated and all pretense of resistance abandoned as the Patriots fled through Savannah and into a swamp on its western edge. The Americans had the choice of drowning, being shot, bayonetted or surrendering. The British captured Savannah, over 500 Americans, and all their artillery at a cost of fewer than 50 men killed and wounded. Fewer than 200 Americans escaped Savannah.

The British rapidly consolidated their hold over Georgia. General Augustine Prevost marched overland from St. Augustine, taking American coastal garrisons as he marched north. At the same time, Campbell started troops up the

After two years of relative peace, war returned to the South in December 1778. The long delay allowed local governments to establish control over their territory but did not eliminate long standing local animosity which often had little to do with the rebellion.

Savannah River and took outlying towns. Once Prevost arrived and took command, Campbell marched on Augusta.

Aided by Thomas Brown, a local Tory returning from Florida exile with a battalion of rangers, Augusta fell without a fight on January 31. The lone setback, a failure to capture Burke County, seemed minor as over a thousand men joined the British in the next two weeks. Word of others coming from as far away as North Carolina suggested the South was ripe for the picking.

Then things began to sour. Andrew Pickens, a South Carolina Patriot from the Long Canes settlements west of Ninety Six, brought his troops into Georgia. North Carolina Tories and South Carolina Patriots clashed at Kettle Creek, Georgia, northwest of Augusta. Pickens was outnumbered but the surprised Tories were routed in a two-hour battle that cost them nearly 200 casualties.

Word of this engagement and of some 4,000 approaching Patriots caused Campbell to abandon Augusta. Even a modest victory at Briar Creek, where Campbell thrashed a Patriot column attempting to cut off the British retreat did not restore Loyalist fervor. The British retreated toward Savannah, leaving outposts along the river. Backcountry Loyalists lost enthusiasm when Augusta was evacuated. After Patriots tried over sixty prisoners for treason and hanged five of them, Tory morale fell even lower.

Patriot reprisals against Tories were vicious and it became clear to royal sympathizers that if the British military presence were not permanent, it was best not to turn out and support the king. The price when the British army moved on was just too high. It was one thing to be in a fighting unit, it was another thing entirely to live in an isolated farmstead when Patriot raiders struck back, whipping, torturing and burning.

A stalemate resulted. The British occupied Savannah; South Carolinians and other Americans held Charles Town. As Patriots tried to pacify the backcountry, Prevost left Savannah and marched on Charles Town. Arriving in mid-May, Prevost called on the town to surrender. The governor and his council proposed that, if the British would spare Charles Town, South Carolina would remain neutral until the war was over and then join the winner. Governor Routledge later claimed he was stalling because help was on the way, but his offer is symptomatic of the disarray among the Americans.

Unable to take the city, Prevost retreated as the main army approached to defend Charles Town. Taking position at Stono Ferry, the British began evacuating to Savannah by boat. The Americans under Benjamin Lincoln attacked on June 20. The attack failed.

The rest of the summer was somewhat quiet as both sides regrouped. In

A TORY RECEIVES HARSH PUNISHMENT FROM PATRIOTS IN THIS 18TH-CENTURY ILLUSTRATION.

(LC)

September, the Americans and their new allies, the French, moved against Savannah. The British garrison was surprised when the French under Vice Admiral Charles-Henri Comte d'Estaing landed troops near Savannah. Had the French attacked immediately, they could have taken the town but political considerations about the new alliance dictated that Savannah be taken by a combined Franco-American force.

The British garrison, sailors, Tories, and hundreds of slaves completed a defensive line around the town. Summoned to surrender, Prevost asked for a day to work out terms. The allies agreed and in those twenty-four hours, British reinforcements under Maitland, the hero of Stono Ferry, reached Savannah. All talk of surrender ceased and a siege began.

For six days, the allies shot up the town. On October 9, 1779, French and Americans stormed the fortifications and failed in a bloody two hour battle. The key point was the Spring Hill Redoubt defended by Tories, including Thomas Brown of Augusta, and Highland Scots of the 71st Regiment.

Despite placing their colors on the parapet, French and American assault parties were driven off with nearly 20 percent casualties. d'Estaing himself was among the wounded. Sergeant Jasper, the

> "We had to march in the open for 425 yards. Then we intended to cross the abatis, jump down into the trench, and clamber up the redoubt. As soon as the English saw us, they set up a very stiff fire against our troops and greatly retarded our march. ... The column was broken down and the first ones to reach the glacis were easily knocked down. The 600 rebels advanced to attack and added to the disorder. ... We took two steps forward and five backward, shouting all the time: "Long live the King!" Those who had overrun the trench were not supported and practically all killed. Some of them climbed up the redoubt from which they were soon dislodged. The troops gave way a little, were rallied, but they advanced only very apathetically. The enemy received reinforcements suddenly. His fire became stiffer, and everyone fled... We had to run away from grapeshot. We were not even safe from cannon in our camp ... The affair lasted fifty-five minutes." — Francois d'Auber de Peyrelongue, French Artillery Officer

An account of the attack upon Savannah under the orders of the Comte d'Estaing from *Muskets, Cannon Balls & Bombs – Nine Narratives of the Siege of Savannah in 1779*. Edited and Translated by Benjamin Kennedy; Behive Press, Savannah, Georgia.

hero of Fort Moultrie (formerly Fort Sullivan, renamed in honor of Colonel William Moultrie) placed his flag on the Spring Hill parapet but fell mortally wounded. A Polish cavalryman, Casimir Pulaski was hit by grapeshot in the hail of gunfire before the redoubt.

The French, fearing the hurricanes so common in the fall, departed and sailed to the Caribbean. The Americans retreated to Charles Town and both sides settled in for the winter. Georgia's coast had been under British control for a year.

## Charles Town

In December, Sir Henry Clinton left New York with additional ships and troops. Using Savannah as a staging area, the British fleet landed troops below Charles Town in mid-February. Clinton moved very slowly but was only seven miles from Charles Town when the fleet sailed past Fort Moultrie and dropped anchor in the harbor. The American commander, Benjamin Lincoln, yielding to pressure from the civilian government, did not evacuate Charles Town.

On April 10, 1780, Clinton summoned the city to surrender. By that time, British approach trenches were already close enough to threaten the town defenses with artillery fire. Four days later, the last escape route was closed off when Lieutenant Colonel James Webster seized Monck's Corner northwest of the town. Lieutenant Colonel Banastre Tarleton, commander of the British Legion, started gaining notoriety as he battered Continental troops around Monck's Corner and, shortly thereafter, at Lenud's Ferry. On April 20, Lincoln proposed that he surrender the town on

# Stono Ferry

The defences of this place consisted of three redoubts ... protected by a common abbatis; some pieces of field artillery filled the intervals, and the redoubts were mounted with cannonades and some howitz, the charge of this important post was committed to Col Maitland — with about 700 men ... Genl Lincoln displayed the Army about 400 yards from the lines of the Enemy, ... the Army advanced in good order, extending the whole length of the Enemy's front — The British reserved their fire till the Americans were within about 60 yds when a General discharge of Musquetry and Artillery completely checked the assailants. The fire was instantly returned, and continued incessantly for 30 minutes, when an effort was made to carry on the men to storm the works, but that moment was passed, and after a pause of a few seconds the fire again commenced on both sides; the attack was continued in this manner for an hour and 20 minutes, when the appearance of a reinforcement and the carnage among the American Troops induced the General to order a retreat, this of course produced some confusion in the front line, and Colo Maitland made a sallie with his whole force. Genl Lincoln ordered the Cavalry to charge the Enemy who were now advancing rapidly in loose order with an irregular; upon this movement the British troops formed and received the cavalry with so firm a countenance and a fire so well directed that these light and ill disciplined troops were immediately dispersed; the reserve of Virginia Militia were now moved forward and commenced a heavy fire on the advance of the British troops, under cover of which the army was again formed, and the retreat effected.

— William R. Davie, Captain, Pulaski's Legion

*The Revolutionary War Sketches of William R. Davie*,
North Carolina Department of Cultural Resources, Raleigh, North Carolina; 1976.

GENERAL BENJAMIN LINCOLN

(NPS)

condition that the Continentals be permitted to keep their arms and march away. Clinton rejected the proposal and began bombarding the town which convinced the city fathers to permit a surrender. Despite the gallant, if hopeless, defense, Clinton refused the garrison the "honors of war," so the Americans had to march out playing an American tune with their colors cased.

Charles Town fell on May 12 with over 5,000 men and 391 artillery pieces falling into British hands. The surrender put virtually all deep south Continentals into prison ships. The militia were paroled and sent home.

THE SIEGE OF CHARLESTON (CHARLES TOWN), 1780

(LC)

WILLIAM MOULTRIE

(NA)

**Buford's command was destroyed and in the ensuing rout, atrocities were committed. Some men suffered multiple bayonet and saber wounds, many of them after they were already prostrated.**

### Waxhaws

Clinton immediately sent troops into the interior to secure the countryside by occupying key outposts. The most rapid movement was led by Lieutenant Colonel Banastre Tarleton and his British Legion who went after the last Continental army remnants in South Carolina. After learning of the surrender of Charles Town, this composite group of Virginians was trying to escape. Not a regiment, these men were led by Abraham Buford. After a brutal 150-mile march in a little over two days, Tarleton's advance caught up with Buford at Waxhaws. Stalling for time while his wagons tried to escape, Buford rejected calls for surrender and formed his men.

What happened next is subject to interpretation but Tarleton pointed out that the Virginians held their fire until the British Legion's cavalry charge was less than ten yards away. The volley staggered the dragoons but momentum carried horses and men into the battle line where the Loyalists began hacking away at the Virginians trying to surrender or escape. Ever since, "Tarleton's Quarter" and "Bloody Tarleton" were synonymous with British cruelty.

Buford's command was destroyed and in the ensuing rout, atrocities were committed. Some men suffered multiple bayonet and saber wounds, many of them after they were already prostrated. At least a hundred Virginians were buried in the next week. Tarleton denied nothing, noting only that his men were not easily restrained.

Within a week, the British issued a proclamation ordering that anyone not actively supporting Loyalist government was an enemy and no longer protected by the army. This was against paroles surrendering militiamen signed at Charles Town and their neutrality was compromised. Either they turned out as Loyalist militia or they became outlaws as far as the British were concerned. This order ignited the backcountry because British militia used it as an excuse to attack Patriot farmsteads and plantations.

## Camden

Even before Charles Town fell, reinforcements were on the way. The Maryland and Delaware Line, eight Continental regiments under Major General, Johann, Baron De Kalb, were just reaching North Carolina when they learned Charles Town had fallen and then heard of Waxhaws. De Kalb pressed on despite supply shortages. In July, the Continentals were joined by General Horatio Gates, the "Hero of Saratoga," who promised better times and then marched them through an area entirely devoid of supplies to threaten Camden, South Carolina.

Joined by Virginia and North Carolina militia, Gates opted for a night march against the British garrison and, lacking rum, issued his men molasses. Coincidentally, Camden's defenders also sallied out that night. Unlike the Americans falling out of ranks all night to ease themselves, Cornwallis' men were ready when they met Gates' advanced

Lieutenant-colonel Tarleton made his arrangement for the attack with all possible expedition ...Captains Corbet and Kinlock were directed, with the 17th dragoons and part of the legion, to charge the center of the Americans; whilst Lieutenant-colonel Tarleton, with thirty chosen horse and some infantry assaulted their right flank and reserve ... On their arrival within fifty paces, the continental infantry presented, when Tarleton was surprised to hear their officers command them to retain their fire till the British cavalry were nearer. This forbearance in not firing before the dragoons were within ten yards of the object of their attack, prevented their falling into confusion on the charge, and likewise deprived the Americans of the farther use of their ammunition: some officers, men, and horses, suffered by this fire; but the battalion was totally broken, and slaughter was commenced before Lieutenant-colonel Tarleton could remount another horse, the one with which he led his dragoons being overturned by the volley. Thus in a few minutes ended an affair which might have had a very different termination. The British troops had two officers killed, one wounded; three privates killed, thirteen wounded; and thirty-one horses killed and wounded. The loss of officers and men was great on the part of the Americans, owing to the dragoons so effectually breaking the infantry, and to a report amongst the cavalry that they had lost their commanding officer, which stimulated the soldiers to a vindictive asperity not easily restrained. Upwards of one hundred officers and men were killed on the spot; three colours, two six-pounders, and above two hundred prisoners, with a number of waggons, ... fell into the possession of the victors.

— Banastre Tarleton, Lieutenant Colonel, British Legion

*A History of the Campaigns of 1780 and 1781 in the Southern Provinces of North America,* T. Cadell, London.

guard at 2:00 A.M. A brief exchange of fire ensued, then both sides prepared for battle when daylight came.

Each army deployed in a similar fashion. Gates put his Continentals on the right, opposite British provincials. Cornwallis placed his regulars in a single rank, with men five-feet apart, opposite American militia. After very little firing, the militia broke and ran, freeing the British regulars to swing left against the Continentals who were driving off the Loyalist provincials. Outnumbered and surrounded, the Continentals fought heroically. De Kalb went down with at least eleven wounds. The largest American contingent leaving the field numbered fewer than a hundred. Gates, on a fine horse, rode to Hillsborough in three days. His Continentals took almost

a month to get there; the militia never did, they simply went home.

Camden was a major tactical disaster for the Americans and encouraged Cornwallis to occupy Charlotte. Camden spurred Congress to allow Washington's choice of a leader for the Southern Army. He chose his old quartermaster, Nathanael Greene. Washington's choice proved to be a disaster for the British.

## Partisan Warfare

Initially, the backcountry was relatively calm after Charles Town fell. Both sides seemed almost willing to wait and see what would happen. Whatever the reasons, Patriots, Tories and outlaw raiders already had chosen their positions. Even though some switching of loyalty, usually for personal gain, occurred as the war went on, most backcountry residents remained true to their economic and social roots; some were longstanding and may predate their families' arrival in the backcountry. Still, it was not surprising when raiding and plundering began as Tories moved to punish Patriots for four years of harassment.

MAJOR GENERAL BARON DE KALB LIES DYING ON THE BATTLEFIELD AT CAMDEN, SOUTH CAROLINA.

(LC)

# The Battle of Camden

It happened that the ground on which both armies stood, was narrowed by swamps on the right and left, so that the Americans could not avail themselves of their superior numbers in outflanking us. We immediately began the attack with great vigor, and in a few minutes the action became general along the whole line; there was a dead calm with a little haziness in the air, which prevented the smoke from rising; this occasioned such thick darkness, that it was difficult to see the effect of the fire on either side. Our army either kept up a constant fire, or made use of their bayonets as opportunity offered. After an obstinate resistance for some time the Americans were thrown into total confusion, and were forced to give way in all quarters. The continental troops behaved well, but some of the militia were soon broken. In justice to the North Carolina militia, it should be remarked, that part of the brigade commanded by General Gregory acquitted themselves well; they were formed immediately on the left of the continentals, and kept the field while they had a cartridge to fire. Gregory himself was twice wounded by a bayonet in bringing off his men; several of his regiment, and many of his brigade who were made prisoners had no wound except from bayonets.

— Roger Lamb, Sergeant, 23rd Foot

*An Original and Authentic Journal of Occurrences during the late American War,* Wilkinson & Courtney, Dublin, Ireland; 1809.

Genl Gates, I presume, has acquainted Congress of the total loss of the Artillery & Baggage, and of most of the muskets that were in the hands of the Militia; these, except one North Carolina Militia Regiment, commanded on the occasion by Col. Dixon of the Regulars, behaved in the most shameful manner. They were drawn up in close order, two deep, the Enemy who opposed them, from a defect in numbers, were only a single file five feet apart, yet the Militia, tho' so much superior in numbers, gave way on the first fire, and fled with the utmost precipitation, notwithstanding every endeavour of their officers to keep them to the charge. I cannot as yet learn what particular Corps fled first; however, the field was soon cleared of all our Army, except the Regulars and the Militia Regiment I mention, who bravely stood and pushed bayonets to the last.

— Abner Nash, Governor of North Carolina

Governor Abner Nash to Delegates in Congress, August 23, 1780; from *North Carolina State Papers, 1776-1788.*

The two armies came near each other at Sutton's about twelve or one o'clock in the night... I remember that I was among the nearest to the enemy; that a man name John Summers was my file leader; that we had orders to wait for the word to commence firing; that the militia were in front and in a feeble condition at that time. They were fatigued. The weather was warm excessively. They had been fed a short time previously on molasses entirely... I believe my gun was the first gun fired, notwithstanding the orders, for we were close to the enemy, who appeared to maneuver in contempt of us, and I fired without thinking except that I might prevent the man opposite from killing me. The discharge and loud roar soon became general from one end of the lines to the other. Amongst other things, I confess I was amongst the first that fled. The cause of that I cannot tell, except that everyone I saw was about to do the same. It was instantaneous. There was no effort to rally, no encouragement to fight.

— Garret Watts, private, North Carolina Militia

*The Revolution Remembered,* University of Chicago Press, Chicago; 1980.

THE BAYONET CHARGE BY THE MARYLAND BRIGADE AT THE BATTLE OF CAMDEN.
(LC)

Following Charles Town's surrender and Tarleton's annihilation of Buford at Waxhaws, things were temporarily settled in South Carolina. A line of British posts ran up the Savannah River to Augusta, then north through Ninety Six, around to Rocky Mount, and east through Camden, Cheraws, to Georgetown. The garrisons seemed to have cowed resistance. Most Patriots gave their paroles, swearing to remain neutral, and returned home.

The British concentrated on organizing their own Loyalist militia and reestablishing order. In the backcountry, the new British militia was formed under Major Patrick Ferguson because he was a good recruiter and trainer. The Loyalists were not required to serve outside the Carolinas or Georgia and men with families remained in their home districts. The militia would maintain order and collect supplies for British garrisons. By early June 1780, South Carolina seemed under control.

The British plan to secure the state behind a line of outposts defended by Loyalist militia was proceeding well until the Tory militia, freed of Patriot dominance, began to settle old scores. The backcountry began to seethe. Civil unrest was encouraged by Clinton's proclamation stating that those who did not serve in the militia were "considered as enemies and rebels."

The proclamation served as an excuse for some Tories to strike back at the Patriots and started paroled Patriots moving toward active resistance once again. The Patriots felt their paroles had been violated because they had initially been told they could remain neutral. After their homes were plundered by Tory raiders, they began to rearm and reassemble into their old units. Several small actions took place in the backcountry as local groups jockeyed for position. By the end of June 1780, it was rapidly becoming clear to the king's men that South Carolina was not pacified and was on the verge of open warfare between Tory and Patriot.

The British Legion reinvigorated American resistance by burning Thomas Sumter's plantation, releasing this key leader from his parole. Sumter became the focal point of Patriot resistance until he was wounded at Blackstocks (November 20, 1780), when the fire seems to have left him. By that time, it made little difference because Francis Marion and then, as 1780 turned into 1781, Andrew Pickens, turned out to lead rebel forces. Sumter, and other partisan leaders including Clarke of Georgia, Shelby and Davie of North Carolina kept things boiling until then.

In July 1780, Patriot leaders caught one raiding party under notorious leader Captain Christian Huck. The Tories were wiped out and Huck killed. Shortly after, North Carolinian William R. Davie attacked the British at Hanging Rock. Davie later reported that, "no prisoners could be safely taken" because a British garrison was a short distance away. "Tarleton's Quarter" was being paid back by equally violent rebels. Davie rarely gave quarter and on occasion issued orders to take no prisoners.

A major turning point in this brutal civil war occurred at Musgrove's Mill, South Carolina, August 18, 1780. Here, about 500 regulars and Loyalist militiamen

were attacked by Carolina militia. What began with an apparent Patriot rout was turned into a disaster as the pursuit entered a killing zone where American fire swept through British ranks. Total British casualties were estimated at over 220 in killed, wounded, and captured. The Patriots suffered only 11 killed and wounded.

When one reviews backcountry casualties, it is clear most engagements were over very quickly; winners had few casualties while losers suffered heavily. Once order and disciplined ranks were no longer maintained, the winners exacted a fearsome toll in the pursuit, hacking away

A BRITISH SOLDIER MURDERS AN AMERICAN PLANTER IN COLDBLOOD.

(LC)

PATRIOT PETER FRANCISCO SINGLE-HANDEDLY FENDS OFF TARLETON'S BRITISH DRAGOONS IN VIRGINIA.

(COURTESY OF ANNE S.K. BROWN MILITARY COLLECTION, BROWN UNIVERSITY)

# The Partisan War

Swords, at first, were scarce, but we had several good blacksmiths among us; besides, there were several in the country. If we got hold of a piece of good steel, we would keep it; and likewise, to all the sawmills, and take all the old whip saws we could find, set three or four smiths to work, in one shop, and take the steel we had, to another. In this way, we soon had a pretty good supply of swords and butcher knives. ...

Our swords and knives, we polished mostly with a grindstone — not a very fine polish to be sure; but they were of a good temper, sharpened to a keen edge, and seldom failed to do execution, when brought into requisition.

We would go to a turner or wheelwright, and get headblocks turned, of various sizes, according to the heads that had to wear them, in shape resembling a sugar loaf; we would then get some strong upper, or light sole leather, cut it out in shape, close it on the block, then grease it well with tallow, and set it before a warm fire, still on the block, and keep turning it round before the fire, still rubbing on the tallow, until it became almost as hard as a sheet of iron; we then got two small straps or plates of steel, made by our own smiths, of a good spring temper, and crossing in the centre above, one reaching from ear to ear, the other, in the contrary direction; the lining was made of strong cloth, padded with wool, and fixed so as to prevent the cap from pressing too hard on the ears; there was a small brim attached to the front ... a piece of bearskin lined with strong cloth, padded with wool, passed over from the front to the back of the head; then a large bunch of hair taken from the tail of a horse, generally white, was attached to the back part and hung down the back; then, a bunch of white feathers, or deer's tail, was attached to the sides, which completed the cap.

— James Collins, Private,
South Carolina Militia

*Autobiography of a Revolutionary War soldier,*
Feliciana Democrat, Clinton, Louisiana; 1859.

SERGEANTS NEWTON AND JASPER OF MARION'S BRIGADE RESCUING AMERICAN PRISONERS, 1778.

(LC)

with sabers. This viciousness continued for eighteen brutal months in the Carolinas. Both sides were guilty of outright murder when the opportunity for retribution presented itself.

Coming as it did immediately after the defeat at Camden, Musgrove's Mill relit the rebellion's fire, even though Thomas Sumter's command was smashed by Tarleton's Legion at Fishing Creek the same day. Other, unintended consequences came when Ferguson learned who the leaders were. Along with Georgians under Elijah Clarke, Patriots at Musgrove's Mill included "overmountain" men from the frontier.

When Clarke attacked but failed to take Augusta, he began a refugee movement into western settlements "over the mountains" with his followers and their families. Ferguson decided to put them out of the war. First, he tried to intercept Clarke. When he failed to catch the Georgia partisan, Ferguson issued a proclamation stating that, if the overmountain rebels did not cease opposing crown forces, he would "hang their leaders and lay their country waste." This was a threat overmountain leaders could understand and they reacted immediately. Word went out along the frontier and by the end of September 1780, over 1,200

The first class of Whigs were those who determined to fight it out to the last let the consequence be what it might; the second class were those who would fight a little when the wind was favorable, but so soon as it shifted to an unfavorable point would draw back and give up all for lost; the third class were those who were favorable to the cause, provided it prospered and they could enjoy the benefit but would not risk one hair of their heads to attain it.

There was a class of Tories who I believe were Tories from principle; another class believed it impossible for the cause of liberty to succeed, and thought in the end, whatever they got, they would be enabled to hold, and so become rich — they resorted to murdering and plunder, and every means to get hold of property; another class were Tories entirely through fear, and fit for nothing only to be made tools of by the others, and all cowards too.

There was another class of men amongst us, who pretended neutrality entirely on both sides... when volunteers would be called for, and by joining them I would be equally safe; if I went to battle I stood as fair a chance; besides I would be less exposed, less fatigued, and if there should be any time of resting, I could come home and enjoy it. — James Collins, private, South Carolina Militia

*Autobiography of a Revolutionary War Soldier,* Feliciana Democrat, Clinton, Louisiana; 1859.

The good will of the inhabitants is absolutely requisite to retain a country after we have conquered it, I fear it will be some time before we can recover the confidence of those in Carolina, as their past sufferings will of course make them cautious of forwarding the King's interests before there is the strongest certainty of his army being in a condition to support them. — Henry Clinton, British General

Letter from General Henry Clinton to Lord George Germain, July 18, 1781.

There were some men in the country conscientiously opposed to war and every sort of revolution which led to it or invoked it aids. They believed that they ought to be in subjection to the powers that be, hence they maintained their allegiance to the British crown. ...

There were many men who knew nothing of the merits of the question at issue. ... fit subjects for demagogues and tyrants. They followed their leaders in 1776 as at other times.

Another class thought the government of George III too good to exchange for an uncertainty.

Another class thought that however desirable the right of self-government might be, it was out of the question unless His Most Gracious Majesty might be pleased to grant it.

There was yet another class. A set of men who give themselves a good deal of credit for shrewdness and management. ... If they ever had

scruples of conscience they amount to very little. ... Upon the whole, the needle is no truer to the pole than they are to the prospect of gain.

There was another class that had a bad representation among the Tories. A class too, which, either on account of its numbers, industry or general influence, gave character to the whole fraternity. ... A pack of rogues. ... now enjoys the liberty of plundering under the sanction of law and of arresting for reward those who have been long known as staunch defenders of honesty and justice. — James H. Saye, South Carolina Minister

1847 Tories Classified, from *Kings Mountain and Its Heroes,* Genealogical Publishing Company, Baltimore.

The crackers and militia in those parts of America are all mounted on horse-back, which renders it totally impossible to force them to an engagement with infantry *only*. When they chuse to fight, they dismount, and fasten their horses to the fences and rails; but if not very confident in the superiority of their numbers, they remain on horse-back, give their fire, and retreat, which renders it useless to attack them without cavalry: for though you repulse them, and drive them from the field, you never can improve the advantage, or do them any material detriment. — George Hanger, Major, British Legion

*An Address to the Army in Reply to Strictures,* by Roderick M'Kenzie; 1789.

men from the Carolina and Virginia settlements gathered at Sycamore Shoals. As Ferguson withdrew, overmountain men pursued. For some reason, Ferguson took refuge on Kings Mountain instead of hastening on to Cornwallis at Charlotte.

## Kings Mountain

Kings Mountain is an isolated high ridge near the North Carolina line. The top was cleared but its steep slopes were heavily wooded. The cleared area served as an excellent camp ground for Ferguson's 1,100 Tory militiamen camping on the northeast end. Early on October 7, the over-

mountain men pushed on through a rain. About 3:00 P.M., the Patriots arrived at the foot of the mountain and prepared for immediate attack.

THE BATTLE OF KINGS MOUNTAIN, BY ALONZO CHAPPEL (LC)

Isaac Shelby and William Campbell took their men to the southwest. The remainder, under Benjamin Cleveland, John Sevier and Joseph McDowell, moved to the northeastern foot of the ridge. Ferguson's outlying posts were taken by surprise and no warning reached the Tories on top of the hill. After silencing the Tory pickets, the Patriots advanced with a war whoop, heading straight up the difficult slope. Ferguson was all over, rallying his men and sending them downslope in spoiling bayonet attacks. The overmountain men recoiled before each attack but then swarmed right back, taking cover at every opportunity and firing into the Tory ranks.

Kings Mountain is unique in that many Patriots were armed with rifles. Their opponents, all Tories, were armed with muskets and bayonets. Another tactical observation is that men shooting downhill tend to fire high while men shooting uphill hit their mark. As the Tories charged, they were exposed to rifle fire at close range. While Tory bayonet attacks were temporarily successful, the Patriots simply moved back, drifting away, taking cover behind rocks and trees, then returning to battle

when the Tories retired to the crest.

Gradually, the Patriots fought their way onto the mountain top. Here, they found a clear vista advantageous to aimed rifle fire. The Tories were almost helpless in the face of such destructive fire. While attempting to rally his men for a charge through encircling riflemen, Ferguson was shot down. Both arms broken, his hat and clothing shot to pieces, Ferguson died as his command disintegrated. Unable to restrain their bloodlust, overmountain men continued shooting, yelling "Tarleton's Quarter," as they swarmed over Loyalists, many of whom threw down their muskets trying to surrender.

The Loyalists lost over 300 killed and wounded, but nearly 700 were taken prisoner. After insulting Ferguson's corpse, the Patriots marched some 16 miles the day following the battle to get their prisoners away. Within a few days, a court martial was held and several of the more notorious Tories were executed at Biggerstaff's Old Fields in what is now modern day Rutherford County, North Carolina. More importantly, when Cornwallis heard of this disaster, he decided to evacuate Charlotte and go into winter quarters at Winnsboro, South Carolina, because he felt his western flank was no longer secure.

## Cowpens

In December 1780, General Nathanael Greene arrived in Charlotte, North Carolina. Within three weeks, he reorganized the Southern Army and divided it into two segments capable of defending themselves while threatening British interests in South Carolina. Greene's main force

# Kings Mountain

I was commanded this day by Major Chronicle and Capt. Watson. We were soon in motion, every man throwing four or five balls in his mouth to prevent thirst, also to be in readiness to reload quick. The shot of the enemy soon began to pass over us like hail; the first shock was quickly over, and for my own part, I was soon in a profuse sweat. My lot happened to be in the centre, where the severest part of the battle was fought. We soon attempted to climb the hill, but were fiercely charged upon and forced to fall back to our first position; we tried a second time, but met the same fate; the fight seemed to become more furious. Their leader, Ferguson, came in full view, within rifle shot as if to encourage his men, who by this time were falling very fast; he soon disappeared. We took to the hill a third time; the enemy gave way; when we had gotten near the top, some of our leaders roared out, "...They are crying for quarter."
— James Collins, Private, South Carolina Militia

*Autobiography of a Revolutionary War Soldier,* Feliciana Democrat, Clinton, Louisiana; 1859.

I well remember how I behaved. Ben Hollingsworth and I took right up the side of the mountain and fought our way from tree to tree up to the summit. I recollect I stood behind one tree and fired until the bark was nearly all knocked off and my eyes pretty well filled with it. One fellow shaved me pretty close, for his bullet took a piece out of my gun-stock. Before I was aware of it I found myself apparently between my own regiment and the enemy, as I judged from seeing the paper which the Whigs wore in their hats, and the pine twigs the Tories wore in theirs.
— Thomas Young, Major, South Carolina Militia

Memoir of Major Thomas Young, 1843.

The action commenced about two o'clock in the afternoon and was very severe for upwards of an hour, during which the Rebels were charged and drove back several times, with considerable slaughter. When our detachment charged, for the first time, it fell to my lot to put a Rebel Captain to death, which I did most effectually, with one blow of my sword; the fellow was at least six feet high, but I had rather the advantage, as I was mounted on an elegant horse, and he on foot. But their numbers enabled them to surround us and the North Carolina regiment, which consisted of about three hundred men. Seeing this, and numbers being out of ammunition, which naturally threw the rest of the militia into confusion, our gallant little detachment, which consisted of only seventy men, exclusive of twenty who acted as dragoons, and ten who drove wagons ... were all killed and wounded but twenty, and those brave fellows were soon crowded into an heap by the militia. — Anthony Allaire, Lieutenant, American Volunteers, Ferguson's Corps

Rivington's *Royal Gazette,* February 1781.

A DIORAMA DISPLAY OF THE BATTLE OF KINGS MOUNTAIN

(NPS)

moved to a winter camp along the Pee Dee River in South Carolina. From Greene's camp, raiders under Francis Marion attacked Georgetown. The other, the Flying Army under General Daniel Morgan, went west and camped along the Pacolet River southeast of modern Spartanburg. Morgan's force threatened Ninety Six and William Washington's raiding Continental dragoons and militia emphasized the threat.

Concern for Ninety Six led General Cornwallis to drive Morgan away. This reaction force was under Banastre Tarleton's command. Tarleton quickly learned that Ninety Six was not in immediate danger. Reinforced, he began operations that culminated in the Battle of Cowpens, the most impressive American tactical demonstration of the war and a battle that started the British army on the road to ruin at Yorktown.

When Morgan learned Tarleton was after him, he consolidated the Flying Army and moved north to a well known road junction providing access to Broad River fords and reinforcements. By moving north and west, he drew Tarleton after him, forcing the British to maneuver through an area already swept clean of readily available food. On the afternoon of January 16, Morgan chose his campsite, deployed the Flying Army for a battle that might be forced upon him, and fed his men. Reinforcements came in that night and Morgan decided to fight at the Cowpens.

When the British arrived in the pre-dawn darkness, Morgan had his Flying Army placed superbly in lines straddling the Green River Road. In the first line, militia riflemen stood in a wide sweeping formation with North Carolinians on the right, Georgians in the center, and South Carolinians on the left. These skirmishers concealed two other lines, stopped the British advance, and forced them to deploy. Tarleton paused, allowing his men a brief rest after their twelve-mile forced march through rough country. The delay gave Tarleton time to see what little he could of the American position and wait for daylight.

Then, Tarleton advanced, deploying more men on both sides of the road. Quickly, he had a line in open order with light infantry on the right, British Legion Infantry in the center and then the 7th Regiment on the left. Two small cannon, three-pounders called gallopers or grasshoppers, were placed, one in the road and one in the middle of the 7th Regiment. Forty dragoons covered each British flank and trotted uphill against the American line with the infantry.

Morgan's second line was composed of South Carolinians, most armed with rifles, under Colonel Andrew Pickens. The majority of these backcountry men had fought in earlier skirmishes; but for most, this was their biggest battle. The American right flank had two battalions from around Spartanburg. The left flank had the Little River Battalion from Laurens County and a

Union County battalion. Their flanks were covered as the skirmishers fell back to the second line.

The first application of Morgan's superb tactical deployment came on the second line. Morgan's South Carolina militia was behind the crest, out of sight of the British and slightly lower downslope. The Laurens County men were a little forward of the line, creating a gap so the skirmishers could withdraw without disrupting the battle line. Then, just before the British came within range, the battalion moved back and filled the gap. As the British came over the slight crest, they were silhouetted against the lightening skyline and would be firing downhill.

Pickens ordered sharpshooters to advance and indicate when their battalions should open fire. At a range of less than forty yards, the preliminary firing began. Then, the British were staggered by five volleys fired in rapid sequence as the South Carolina rifles lashed the British front in less than a minute. According to one British leader, over half the British officers and nearly that many men went down from this fire.

Despite their losses, the redcoats pressed forward with their bayonets and broke the militia line. As the center battalions went to the rear, flankers conducted a fighting withdrawal to the main line. The South Carolinians poured through gaps specifically designed to allow rearward movement without disrupting the main line's ranks.

The main, or third line was com-

INTERPRETERS AT COWPENS REENACT THE CONTINENTAL LINE ATTACK.

(COURTESY OF THE ARTHUR AND HOLLY MAGILL ESTATE)

posed of a solid core of Continental infantry. Four sixty-man companies were from Maryland and Delaware. To the left stood a battalion of Virginia militia augmented by flanking North Carolinians and skirmishers. On the right was another Virginia battalion with Virginia Continentals, Virginia State Troops and militia, plus some North Carolina militia. In front of the right flank, North Carolina skirmishers were still firing on the British.

The two lines engaged in an obstinate firefight for less than ten minutes. To break this deadlock, Tarleton sent cavalry against both American flanks. The 17th Light Dragoons broke through the skirmishers, smashed reforming militia, and scattered them. On the right, more dragoons, supported by the 71st Regiment (Fraser's Highlanders), broke through, and then galloped toward the American rear. Battle episodes occurred in rapid sequence now.

William Washington's 82 Continental Light Dragoons, augmented by perhaps as many as 100 mounted militia, routed the British attacking the South Carolina militia,

# Rifles and Muskets

British and Americans used very similar weapons and the most common for infantry, were muskets. Specialized troops and many frontiersman often used rifles. The differences between rifle and musket were important because they affected how troops carrying them fought.

A musket was a smoothbore, flintlock weapon. The British musket, the famous Brown Bess, fired a ball about three quarters of an inch in diameter. While the Americans used a variety of muskets, during the 1780s most carried French models firing a ball slightly smaller than the British. To increase lethal striking power, both sides used a cartridge called buck and ball containing a large ball and three buck shot, about .30–.35 caliber.

The musket was loaded from prepared paper cartridges containing powder and bullet. The cartridge was torn open and some powder poured into a pan alongside the barrel. The remaining powder was placed into the barrel from the front end, then the ball and buckshot were dropped into the barrel. The balls were rammed down the barrel until they were at the breech.

To shoot, the musket was cocked, aimed at the enemy and fired. When the trigger was pulled, the hammer moved forward and the flint caused sparks to fly into the pan, igniting the priming charge. The priming flared up and the flames went through a hole into the barrel, setting off the main charge and propelling the bullets. A skilled soldier could fire, reload and fire again at least three times in a minute, but firing was generally slower because the army's musketmen fired volleys on command.

The musket had an auxiliary weapon attached to it called the bayonet. This triangular piece of metal was about 18 inches long with a socket to fit over the barrel. The bayonet was used offensively, almost as if it were a spear, and provided a defense against both infantry and cavalry when the musket was unloaded. In both attack and defense, the bayonet required discipline to maintain the ranks presenting a solid wall of steel.

While the musket was described as inaccurate by many people, including Banastre Tarleton's second in command George Hanger, this is not necessarily true. Hanger actually said that practice was everything. Well drilled musketmen, given practice and encouraged to fire rapidly, can deliver fast and accurate fire. Unfortunately, few infantrymen had that extensive practice.

The rifle was a much more specialized weapon. Its defining feature was the barrel which had twisting grooves (rifling) cut into the inside. The grooves caused the bullet to spin which meant that the bullet was more accurate.

Loading the rifle was more complicated. The main powder charge was poured into the barrel. Then a greased piece of cloth was placed over the muzzle and the bullet pushed into the cloth, wrapping the patch around the bullet and forming a seal between bullet and barrel. The patched ball was then rammed to the breech. The priming charge was placed in the pan and the rifle could be fired.

The tightly patched ball meant that loading was somewhat slower than a musket but the increased accuracy and longer range gave riflemen an opportunity to strike at a distance well beyond muskets. Instead of firing at men 25-40 yards off, a rifleman could hit targets over 100 yards with ease.

American rifles were personal weapons, made by different gunsmiths and firing many different ball sizes. Consequently, men were issued lead and made their own bullets in a mold specifically fit to their rifle. A rifle could not mount a bayonet because the end of the barrel was often larger than its diameter behind the sight. The sight would be damaged by a socket that slid over the barrel. Riflemen were thus at a disadvantage if they all volley fired together because they could not defend themselves. Consequently, by 1777, most riflemen fought as skirmishers where they could take cover. They also fired aimed shots at specific targets instead of volley fire.

The long range and accuracy created a fearsome reputation among musketmen who felt that rifles were unfair. The British leadership allegedly felt riflemen took great delight in shooting down officers. Still, both sides employed rifles to advantage. In pitched battles during the Southern Campaigns, rifles affected the outcome in three crucial battles, in part because three of the most famous Revolutionary War riflemen were involved.

At Kings Mountain, American "overmountain men," most of whom were armed with rifles, shot up and defeated a musket-armed Loyalist force led by Patrick Ferguson. Ferguson was the inventor of a sophisticated breech loading rifle that could use a bayonet. After he had been wounded in the north, his rifle corps was disbanded and he could not fire a rifle because his arm was crippled. Three years later, this brilliant innovator went to his death commanding musketmen against rifles.

At Cowpens, Daniel Morgan, an accomplished rifleman, very shrewdly placed his riflemen in positions where they could accomplish great damage but retreat if pressed. After skirmishing and then firing by volley, the riflemen ran behind bayonet armed Continentals for protection while they regrouped. Their aimed volley fire caused a significant number of casualties.

The British used foreign riflemen, generally German hunters and foresters called jagers against the Americans from 1776 until the end of the war. The jagers had well deserved reputations for accuracy and military discipline that made them formidable foes.

The British also used Tory riflemen against Americans, in part because they were influenced by George Hanger, the Earl Colraine. Hanger was second in command of Tarleton's British Legion and very interested in the American rifles. He made numerous observations about them and compared them unfavorably to muskets.

At Hobkirk's Hill, when Continental infantry tried to counterattack against advancing British, South Carolina Tories killed at least one Maryland company commander at fairly long range, causing the line to waver, then withdraw. Ultimately, the Americans left the field without ever really coming to close grips, but the initial disruption was caused by riflemen shooting down a key officer.

COLONEL BANASTRE TARLETON

(LC)

then wheeled about and reformed, charging to the right flank where they routed advancing British Legion troopers. The North Carolina skirmishers who sacrificed themselves on the right flank delayed the British less than three minutes, but they bought time for Washington to deal with threats on both flanks and get him into position to help crush all British resistance.

While the cavalry maneuvered, the Continentals proved every bit as good as the British regulars. Tarleton's flank attacks caused them a problem as the 71st swung into line opposite the Americans and fired a volley. The right company, Virginia Continentals, was ordered to swing back but fell into confusion as the Highlanders' volley struck home. In order to maintain order, the Virginians marched rearward. The next company lost their commander and several men in the same Scottish volley. Not understanding what was intended,

they also withdrew. The withdrawal moved down the line as company after company fired, faced about and moved rearward.

Morgan was furious when he saw the withdrawal. However, his second in command, John Eager Howard, pointed out that the men were under control as they marched off. Each company reloaded as they moved rearward with Highlanders shouting war cries behind them. Morgan picked a spot about 100 yards behind the original line as a rally point. Here the Americans stopped, faced about and fired a series of volleys. Howard ordered a bayonet charge that swept away the last organized British units as another American cavalry charge sabered the breaking redcoated infantry.

American cavalry pursued over twelve miles before losing the trail. On their way, they captured numerous supply wagons and fleeing soldiers. Morgan reorganized rapidly to get both prisoners and the Flying Army to safety. The prisoners were sent into North Carolina and the army followed. Morgan sent his militia home, escorting the prisoners as they did

THE BATTLE OF COWPENS BY CHARLES MCBARRON

(NPS)

so; their enlistments were long since up. The Continentals marched, covering the prisoners against the expected British pursuit.

Morgan won a shattering victory. His men did all he asked of them and he had been lucky. Washington's rapid movements thwarted dire threats on both flanks. Howard's superb infantry held the line, then maintained their discipline as they withdrew. When the British became disorganized by pursuit, Howard's volleys smashed them and Washington rode them down. Washington's dragoons were screaming "Buford's Play" as they rode down fleeing British infantry. The British lines were broken and the cavalry had nothing to fear from them. It was all over in less than an hour.

Miles away, the main army with Greene at Cheraw celebrated upon learning of the victory. Then Nathanael Greene started them north. Greene and his bodyguard rode across country and joined Morgan on the Catawba River. Greene and Morgan left for Salisbury the same day, leaving several hundred North Carolina militia under William Lee Davidson to guard the river crossings.

### Race to the Dan

Cornwallis' pursuit was delayed by rain swollen rivers. While examining American positions along the Catawba,

Cornwallis turned his entire army into light troops. The British burned wagons and destroyed extra equipment, then set out after Morgan. This initiated the first phase of the "Race to the Dan" as the Americans covered their prisoners' withdrawal and delayed the British. In effect, the chase was a series of sprints to major river crossings followed by short rests and a renewal of pursuit. Cornwallis moved rapidly but, in lightening his army for forced marching, he destroyed essential supplies that could not be obtained in the wake of the American withdrawal. The British pursued and got very close but never caught the Americans and never recovered their lost men.

Cornwallis crossed his army at Cowans Ford, killing General William Lee Davidson in the process. Tarleton, pressing ahead, scattered militia and so intimidated local citizenry that no one turned out to oppose them. Greene evacuated Salisbury, removing military stores, prisoners, and sick Continentals. Cornwallis, hot on the trail, reached Salisbury as Greene was crossing the Yadkin a few miles ahead. By the time British General Charles O'Hara reached Trading Ford after a rainy night march, Greene was across and the river was rising. The Americans marched on to Guilford Courthouse while Cornwallis was forced to turn north to cross at the Shallow Ford.

The two American armies reunited at Guilford Courthouse on February 8. Here, with the prisoners secure in Virginia, Greene examined the terrain thinking of offering battle. The physical condition of his men and their equipment were not up to providing effective resistance so Greene opted to move north. Morgan, ill, suffering from "sciatica" and other ailments, was given a furlough and went home.

Greene now turned Morgan's army

into a "Flying Army," a fast-moving corps of light infantry under Otho Holland Williams. Cornwallis, knowing the prisoners were beyond his reach, tried to cut off the American rear guard. This second phase of the Race to the Dan was a narrow escape for Greene's Continentals. The British advance was almost within sight of the American rear guard virtually the entire time.

As the main army marched north, Williams' light infantry interceded to block the roads between the two armies. A series of quick, nasty skirmishes took place between advancing British and the American rear. The light infantry conducted their march by sidling north-northeast, convincing Cornwallis that Dix's Ferry was the crossing point. At the last minute, Williams marched east, crossing downstream at Boyd's Ferry on boats commandeered up and down the Dan River.

This withdrawal was a very effective movement. The Americans swept the countryside clean of essential food and forage. Over the last twenty-four hours, Cornwallis marched his entire army over forty miles and still failed to catch Williams' decoy or the main army. They marched

With the promise of reinforcements to come, Greene moved his army back into North Carolina and began alternately threatening the British and tempting them to advance. This period was marked by increased contact between the two antagonists. Several sharp skirmishes at Alamance Creek, Wetzel's Mill, other little road junctions and farmsteads only showed the combatants that each was a very dangerous opponent. Skirmishing was accompanied by the Americans maneuvering west and north of High Rock Ford, a local landmark and Haw

into Hillsborough, raised the British flag, and called on Loyalists to join the cause. Cornwallis' rank and file troops were exhausted and beginning to suffer from lack of adequate food. When Loyalists saw the worn out shoes and tattered clothing, they were not enthusiastic about supporting, much less enlisting, under Cornwallis.

Hillsborough offered no respite because American light infantry, dragoons and mounted militia began attacking British foraging parties. Eventually Cornwallis withdrew westward, into an area he felt offered both supplies and man-power but Guilford County's productivity was marginal because it already had been traversed by both armies. The pacifist nature of its Moravian and Quaker residents did not bode well for turning out many enlistees for the British.

One large group of North Carolina Loyalists under Colonel John Pyle did answer the call, but was intercepted by "Light-Horse Harry" Lee's Legion and cut to pieces. Adding insult to injury, Pyle's Loyalist survivors were fired upon by British sentries when they sought shelter with Cornwallis. After this incident, recruits were even harder to find.

The corps of Williams held a respectable distance, to thwart, as far as was practicable, the nocturnal assault. The duty, severe in the day, became more so at night; for numerous patrols and strong pickets were necessarily furnished by the light troops, not only for their own safety, but to prevent the enemy from placing himself, by a circuitous march, between Williams and Greene. Such a manoeuvre would have been fatal to the American army; and, to render it impossible, half of the troops were alternately appropriated every night to duty: so that each man, during the retreat, was entitled to but six hours' repose in forty-eight. ... The troops were in fine spirits and good health; delighted with their task and determined to prove themselves worthy the distinction with which they had been honored. At the hour of three, their toils were renewed; for Williams always pressed forward with the utmost dispatch in the morning, to gain such a distance in front as would secure breakfast to his soldiers, their only meal during this rapid and hazardous retreat. So fatigued was officer and solider, and so much more operative is weariness than hunger, that each man not placed on duty surrendered himself to repose as soon as the night position was taken.

— Henry Lee, Lieutenant Colonel, Lee's Legion

*Memoirs of the War in the Southern Department of the United States,* Burt Franklin, New York. Originally published in 1812.

River crossing with large open fields on its east bank. Here, Greene awaited reinforcements, reorganized, trained his men, and issued food and ammunition. On March 14, Greene advanced to Guilford Courthouse, fed his men and waited for Cornwallis.

## Guilford Courthouse

Finally, after nearly six weeks of maneuvering across the Carolinas, Greene and Cornwallis decided the issue at a county seat road junction called Guilford Courthouse.

In some ways, Greene followed Morgan's Cowpens deployment but with significant differences. The New Garden Road (Great Salisbury Road) ran east-west through the American positions, bisecting the battlefield. The first American line, mainly comprised of North Carolina militiamen, stood behind a rail fence bordering plowed fields. Ridges extending forward

flanked both sides of the fields. The second line, two Virginia militia brigades, stood on a plateau, flatter ground covered with trees and brush, a half mile back. Farther along, Continental infantry occupied a slope facing a narrow, steep sided vale. The flanks were covered by light troops, including Continental Light Dragoons, infantry, and riflemen. Well ahead of the battlefield, Lee's Legion, augmented by Virginia riflemen and Continentals, were positioned to delay the British.

The battle actually began near New Garden Meeting House about four miles away as advanced elements skirmished. Around 12:30, British infantry deployed, facing the militia across plowed fields, and began marching forward, uphill, under artillery fire. American riflemen on the ridges paralleling the fields opened up at long range, an enfilading fire that caused casualties. This fire proved so disturbing a British battalion moved to the northern

GREENE ENCOURAGES HIS MEN AT GUILFORD COURTHOUSE.

(PAINTING BY DALE GALLON, COURTESY OF DALE GALLON HISTORICAL ART, INC.)

fired one volley, then withdrew in haste as the British infantry charged with bayonets.

Pushing onto the plateau, British infantry battalions broke up, separating into platoons and squads as they approached the second line in the thick brush. Fighting between Virginians and British occurred between small groups groping blindly in the woods; by all accounts it was bitterly contested. Cornwallis had at least one horse shot from under him. Later he was rescued by the 23rd Regiment's Sergeant Lamb.

The Virginia right flank units were confused by conflicting orders. The battalion along the road advanced, leaving both flanks uncovered. The Virginians were struck and then rolled up by the British. The breakthrough spread as the Virginia militia withdrew after heavy fight-

ridge and along it, clearing out riflemen and forcing Kirkwood's Delaware Continentals to retreat. On the southern ridge, the riflemen were pursued only after the first line collapsed. The front line militia

The colonel rode to the front, and gave the word "Charge." Instantly the movement was made, in excellent order, in a smart run, with arms charged: when arrived within forty yards of the enemy's line, it was perceived that their whole force had their arms presented, and resting on a rail fence.... They were taking aim with the nicest precision... At this awful period a general pause took place; both parties surveyed each other for the moment with the most anxious suspense.... colonel Webster rode forward in the front of the 23d regiment, and said, with more than even his usual commanding voice ... "Come on, m brave Fuzileers." This operated like an inspiring voice, they rushed forward amidst the enemy's fire' dreadful was the havoc on both sides. — Roger Lamb, Sergeant, 23rd Regiment

*An Original and Authentic Journal of Occurrences during the late American War,* Wilkinson & Courtney, Dublin, Ireland; 1809.

AMERICAN CAVALRY UNDER THE COMMAND OF
HENRY LEE FIGHT THE BRITISH AT GUILFORD
COURTHOUSE.

(LC)

and, when they encountered Continentals at different times, they were outgunned. The 33rd Regiment under Brigadier General James Webster charged across the little valley and was driven back in a hail of musket and artillery fire. The Continentals pursued them with bayonets but went back to their original positions when the British occupied unassailable steep high ground west of the vale.

D uring this excitement the von Bose Regiment pulled out of the battle line and pursued the enemy, but before we knew it, the enemy attacked us again, in the rear. The regiment therefore, had to divide into two parts. The second, commanded by Major Scheer, had to attack toward the rear against the enemy who were behind us, and forced them once again to take flight. Lord Tarleton came with his Light Cavalry and pursued the enemy. ... During this time Colonel DuBuy advanced with the first part of the regiment and Major Scheer returned ... and rejoined.

— Sergeant Koch, Regiment von Bose

*Enemy Views: The American Revolutionary War as Recorded by the Hessian Participants,* Heritage Books, Bowie, Maryland; 1996.

We repulsed them again; and they a second time made us retreat back to our first ground, where we were deceived for reinforcement of Hessians, whom we took for our own [i.e., continentals], and cried to them to see if they were our friends and shouted LIBERTY! LIBERTY! and advanced up till they let off some guns; then we fired sharply on them, and made them retreat a little. But presently their light horse came on us, and not being defended by our own light horse, nor reinforced, ... we were obliged to run and many were sore chased, and some cut down.

— Rev. Sam Houston, Rifleman, Virginia Militia

*Sketches of Virginia, Historical and Biographical,* J. B. Lippincott, Philadelphia; 1855.

ing. Ferocity on the Virginians' left was, in part, due to General Edward Steven's ordering riflemen behind the line to shoot any men who tried to run. The Virginia stand created disorder in the redcoated battle line now advancing by companies, platoons, and squads, moving forward to drive opponents through the brush. Linear coordination and unit cohesion broke down.

On the far right, two British battalions moved away, fighting American militia and light infantry as they diverged farther and farther from the main battle because the ridges run southeast. The confused fighting created problems for both sides as they mistook each other and were shot up.

The breakup of the British battle line caused by the natural obstructions and differing levels of opposition meant single, unsupported units pushed ahead

The fighting was close, intense and bitter, neither yielding. As the struggling melee moved toward a key land feature, Cornwallis ordered his artillery to fire into the ruck and break it up.

The twenty third and thirty third British regiments under Webster formed the left wing of the British line. They advanced in line with Leslie who commanded the right wing. ... the yagers, light infantry and 33d regt were driven from their ground across the ravine, by Lynch['s] riflemen, Kirkwood's infantry and a charge by Washington's horse and Webster formed them there at right angles with the 23d and to the rear. In this strong position, Webster acted on the defensive behind held completely in check and the action nearly ceased. The 23d Regt which was on Webster's right advanced in front of the "1" Maryland or Gunby's regiment but their attack was feeble and it is evident that Webster's left was held in check it was deemed hazardous to push forward the 23d.... The Guards made their attack on the 2d Maryland Regiment and pursued into the woods directly in the rear and about 60 yards from Gunby's regiment where they took the artillery. Gunby immediately ordered his men to face about and the guards were thrown into confusion, as Cornwallis says, by a heavy fire. As Gunby's Regiment advanced up the hill — Major Anderson was killed & Gunby's horse killed and fell on his leg which threw him behind. Washington's Cavalry ... made the charge upon the guards at the time the first regiment had nearly closed with them. They were pursued into the cleared ground & prostrated by the horse, the infantry following killed and wounded many and brought off some prisoners but many of those whom the horse had prostrated were not much hurt as they fired at us as we left the ground.

— John Eager Howard, Lieutenant Colonel, First Maryland

1804 Letter from John Eager Howard to John Marshall, collections of the Maryland Historical Society, Baltimore, Maryland.

THE AMERICAN CAVALRY MONUMENT

(NPS)

As the Marylanders returned, the British Second Battalion of Guards came into the open ground north of the New Garden Road. They crossed the swale and charged the 2nd Maryland. This unfortunate group originally faced south to cover fields in front of the courthouse. As the southern facing companies wheeled right to oppose the Guards, they were halted, ordered to charge and then halted a second time. Conflicting orders created so much confusion that they broke when the Guards charged.

Fortunately for the Americans, Lieutenant Colonel William Washington, moving behind the Continental battle line, brought his Light Dragoons into the fight and charged the Guards. The First Maryland, screened by a tree line, fired into the Guards' left flank from the rear and charged with bayonets. The initial volleys were so close, flashes from the musket muzzles overlapped.

The clash was a standoff. On one side was perhaps the finest American regiment produced during the war, the First

Maryland Regiment, made up of the surviving remnants of the old Maryland/Delaware Line, men with long service led by outstanding officers. The British troops were the Guards, the British Army's elite troops. The fighting was close, intense and bitter, neither yielding. As the struggling melee moved toward a key land feature, Cornwallis ordered his artillery to fire into the ruck and break it up. When both sides recoiled, Greene, to keep his force intact, began withdrawing as additional redcoat battalions approached and the reformed regiments assaulted across the vale again.

British pursuit was limited and stopped a mile later. The American army survived but lost four cannon. British losses, especially among officers, sergeants, and corporals, came close to crippling Cornwallis' force. Greene camped at Troublesome Creek Ironworks a short distance away; Cornwallis camped on the field he had won at such a price. Wounded suffered terribly in the freezing rain that fell overnight. American morale was high; the British were downcast as news of their losses spread.

BAYONET CHARGE OF THE 1ST MARYLAND REGIMENT AGAINST BRITISH GUARDS AT GUILFORD COURTHOUSE.

(*TURNING POINT AT GUILFORD* BY DALE GALLON, COURTESY OF DALE GALLON HISTORICAL ART, INC.)

REPLICA OF SIX-POUNDER CANNON USED AT GUILFORD BY GREENE'S ARTILLERY.

(NPS)

Smith and his men were in a throng, killing the Guards and Grenadiers like so many Furies. Colonel Stewart [sic], seeing the mischief Smith was doing, made up to him through the crowd, dust and smoke, and made a violent lunge at him with his small sword.... It would have run through his body but for the haste of the Colonel, and happening to set his foot on the arm of a man Smith had just cut down, his unsteady step, his violent lunge, and missing his aim brought him down to one knee on the dead man. The Guards came rushing up very strong. Smith had no alternative but to wheel around and give Stewart [sic] a back-handed blow over, or across the head, on which he fell.

His orderly sergeant attacked Smith, but Smith's sergeant dispatched him. A second attacked him; Smith hewed him down. A third behind him threw down a cartridge and shot him in the back of the head. Smith now fell among the slain, but was taken up by his men and brought off. It was found to be only a buck shot lodged against the skull and had only stunned him.

— Samuel Mathis, post-war business partner of Captain John Smith

Letter from Samuel Mathis to William R. Davie, dated June 26, 1819. Manuscript on file, Historic Camden, Camden, South Carolina.

## THE SOUTH REDEEMED — 1781

After Guilford Courthouse, Cornwallis and Greene moved in different directions. Cornwallis, with little choice, marched to Wilmington, North Carolina — the closest base of supplies and relief — to refit his force. Cornwallis saw the Chesapeake region, especially Virginia, as the key to the lower south. "Until Virginia is in a manner subdued, our hold of the Carolinas must be difficult, if not precarious." To cut off supplies flowing south he wanted to conduct a full scale offensive in Virginia.

Cornwallis felt his northern thrust was a reasonable alternative because a strong British presence remained in South Carolina and Greene just might follow him into Virginia. The end of Cornwallis' campaign occurred when he surrendered at Yorktown in October.

Greene marched into South Carolina where he started reestablishing American control. The "Fighting Quaker" had several things in his favor. While British forces numbered over eight thousand men, they were dispersed in small, scattered garrisons. The Patriot partisans were gathering strength, striking isolated garrisons and supply trains. Finally, the British were not certain where to concentrate even though a mobile force numbering about 2,000 men was available to oppose Greene and reinforcements were on the way. The British lack of focus aided American efforts throughout the summer of 1781. When late fall came, the British were limited to minor coastal posts between garrisons at Charles Town and Savannah.

Greene's plan was based on the premise that, if he kept his Continentals in the field, partisans could delay, divide and defeat the British. Greene cooperated with, and tried to coordinate, the partisan militia. He was most successful with Francis Marion and Andrew Pickens, as Sumter seemingly had his own agenda. Greene maneuvered against major garrisons but kept the British off balance by sending Marion and Pickens, often augmented by Continental detachments against the smaller posts. While major forces engaged in two battles and a siege, partisans destroyed the infrastructure on which the British depended for resupply and Loyalist support.

Ultimately, without winning a single battle himself, Greene won the war of posts, giving credence to the notion that "amateurs study tactics, professionals study logistics." Greene, a former quartermaster general under Washington, understood, perhaps as no one else did, that keeping his army fed and in the field would lead to victory. In offering battle, Greene forced the British to come to him. Coupled with failing supplies, summer heat, and partisan raiding, crown efforts were doomed if they did not destroy Greene's main force and hold their garrison posts.

When Greene marched into South Carolina, the British had four large garrisons strategically placed in a wide arc around the coastal enclaves at Charles Town and Savannah from which they controlled the countryside. These were at Augusta, Ninety Six, Camden, and Georgetown. Not only did they serve as points to recruit Loyalist support but they were also positions from which expeditions were sent into the countryside to gather food and ensure order.

## Hobkirk's Hill

Greene first threatened Camden, the keystone of the British defensive arch. The town was too strong to assault, but it was vulnerable if supplies were cut off. Greene set up camp two miles away and began intercepting foraging parties. The British commander at Camden was Lieutenant Colonel, Francis, Lord Rawdon, an experienced commander. Present at Bunker Hill in 1775, he'd seen service ever since. A capable field commander with an auda-

cious streak, Rawdon did not sit idly when Greene moved against him. His first chance to deal with Greene came in late April. Faced with a threatening American presence, he attacked on April 25.

Rawdon's movement by a side road should have placed the British on the American left flank but the British advance came out forward of the American line. The Continentals, having just eaten, were cleaning kettles and clothing. Some senior officers were even washing their feet. While an advance party fought a skillful delaying action, artillery was brought up, lines were formed and wagons sent to the rear.

Greene waited until Rawdon's infantry came within artillery range, then uncovered his guns. Once engaged, four Continental regiments advanced on line, the two center regiments charging with bayonets. The two flank regiments extended beyond the British line, but as the line moved forward, Loyalist riflemen shot down two Continental officers.

The fickleness of war deprived Greene of victory. When Captain William Beatty, commanding the First Maryland's right flank, was killed, his company halted. Without leadership, confusion soon spread. When ordered to reform, the regiment retired. Rallied, they resumed fighting but the chance was gone.

Even though William Washington disrupted the British rear and captured numerous officers, Greene withdrew to ensure his army's safety. The American artillery was nearly captured but Captain John Smith led a company of Light Infantry into the fray and, with William Washington's help, hauled the guns to safety. In this action, Smith was captured and his company suffered heavy casualties.

Despite the surprise British attack, the Americans fought well. Greene felt this was one battle he should have won and was chagrined when the fighting went against him. Nevertheless, the British soon destroyed their fortifications, evacuated Camden, and for the first time, burned local mills, before moving closer to Charles Town.

When Greene occupied Camden, his army was between British garrisons. The outer British line was in danger of collapse. Greene then moved against Ninety Six in conjunction with partisan raids against outposts and a secondary assault on Augusta, Georgia.

On the twenty-fifth the enemy made a sally out of Camden and were down on our picquet before discovered. At this time our men were, for the chief part, some washing their clothes, and some were out in the country on passes. The first that discovered the enemy were a small picquet belonging to the light infantry, under the command of Captain Kirkwood. As soon as the sentinels discovered them, they fired on them, and gave the alarm; upon which the light infantry immediately turned out and engaged them very vigorously for some time, but, being overpowered by the superiority of their numbers, they retreated about two hundred yards across the main road, where the main picquet of our army was formed ... By this time our main army was drawn up, and engaged them with both cannon and small arms ... Colonel Washington with his cavalry, who, falling in with their rear, killed and wounded a great number of them, making two hundred and fifty of them prisoners. Our main army, being in some confusion by this time by the enemy taking them in flank, retreated off, leading the enemy masters of the field, which, however, they very dearly bought.

— William Seymour, Sergeant Major, First Delaware

*A Journal of the Southern Expedition 1780-1783,*
Historical Society of Delaware, Wilmington, Delaware.

## Ninety Six

Ninety Six had been involved in revolutionary struggle since the earliest days of the conflict. After Charles Town fell, the British occupied the town and improved its fortifications. The expansive Ninety Six district included all upper and western portions of South Carolina. It served as Patrick Ferguson's base while he recruited the Tory militia that was wiped out at Kings Mountain. Located in close proximity to Patriot and Loyalist factions along the river drainage systems, it was *the* backcountry outpost.

Ninety Six was garrisoned by provin-

cial troops from New York and New Jersey, local militiamen, and black pioneers, perhaps 550 all told, under John Harris Cruger, an able New Jersey Loyalist with a lot to lose if Ninety Six fell. The Loyalists had improved and expanded the defenses and knew relief forces could reach them if they held out long enough.

Greene arrived in front of Ninety Six on May 22 and his chief engineer, Colonel Thaddeus Kosciuszko, was amazed at the strength of the fortifications. On one side was the Star Fort, an earthen redoubt with a deep ditch controlling high ground outside the town. On the other side was the Stockade Fort, a palisaded work with timber and brush obstructions extending outward. The alert garrison could not be carried by assault. The situation was more critical than it seemed. With Pickens and Lee in front of Augusta, Greene had less than 500 Continentals, a few more than 400 Virginia militiamen and some North Carolina volunteers. The odds were hardly favorable for a battle, much less assaulting a heavily fortified position.

THE RECREATED
STOCKADE FORT AT
NINETY SIX NHS

(NPS)

Once within striking distance, Kosciuszko directed Greene's men to dig a tunnel to blow up the Star Fort's wall and tried to cut off the water supply. Slaves with buckets were sent out by the Loyalist defenders but water was in short supply. The mine was attacked by the defenders and Kosciuszko was wounded by a bayonet. Ninety Six still held out.

British reinforcements under Lieutenant Colonel Francis Rawdon were marching from Charles Town. Greene ordered Sumter to slow Rawdon's march, but the Gamecock took his time getting into position and Rawdon got past him. Six days after leaving Charles Town, Rawdon was close enough to get word into Ninety Six.

By then Augusta had fallen and Greene ordered those men and supplies to Ninety Six. The Americans, with time running out, tried taking the post by assault before Rawdon could relieve it. Lee's Legion, fresh from the victory at Augusta, would assault the Stockade Fort while Continentals tried to take the Star Fort.

On June 18, the two pronged attack

Following Kosciuszko's advice, Greene opted for a siege, digging trenches closer and closer to the fortifications. The first trenches were placed only 70 yards away, so the British sallied out, captured the entrenching tools and inflicted a humiliating setback. New trenches were opened at the more respectable distance of 200 yards from the Star Fort. To keep down the fort's defenders, a thirty-foot-tall log tower was built and rifle fire picked off anyone so unwise as to show himself.

ATTACK ON THE STAR FORT AT NINETY SIX

(PAINTING BY ROBERT WILSON, COURTESY OF NINETY SIX CHAMBER OF COMMERCE)

Rawdon continued to advance by forced marches.... In this effort he completely succeeded, and ... It now became necessary to hazard an assault, to meet Rawdon, or to retire. ... Orders were issued to prepare for storming; and the hour of twelve, on the next day (18th of June), was appointed... Lieutenants Duval, of Maryland, and Seldon, of Virginia, commanded the forlorn hope of Campbell, and Captain Rudolph, of the Legion, that of Lee. Fascines were prepared to fill up the enemy's ditch; long poles with iron hooks were furnished to pull down the sand-bags, ... The first signal was announced from the centre battery, upon which the assailing columns entered the trenches, manifesting delight in the expectation of carrying by their courage the great prize in view. At the second cannon, which was discharged at the hour of twelve, Campbell and Lee rushed to the assault. Cruger, always prepared, received them with his accustomed firmness. The parapets were manned with spike and bayonet, and the riflemen, fixed at the sand-bag apertures, maintained a steady and destructive fire. Duval and Seldon entered the enemy's ditch at different points, and Campbell stood prepared to support them in the rear of the party furnished with hooks to pull down the sandbags. This party had also entered the enemy's ditch, and began to apply the hook. ... Major Greene, commanding in the star redoubt, ... determined to try the bayonet in his ditch as well as on his parapet.

— Henry Lee, Lieutenant Colonel, Partisan Legion

*Memoirs of the War in the Southern Department of the United States,* Burt Franklin, New York. Originally published in 1812.

hit Ninety Six. The Stockade Fort fell quickly but the "forlorn hope" assigned to assault the Star Fort were not successful. The attackers, armed with hooks to pull down sandbags, muskets, and bayonets were stopped in the fort ditch. The walls were too high and the defenders sallied out, coming around in the ditch from both sides. Thirty of the fifty soldiers in the "forlorn hope" were killed or wounded.

On June 19, Greene retreated after conducting the longest siege of the American Revolution (28 days). Ninety Six stood the test and held out until relieved. When Rawdon got to Ninety Six, his men were too worn out from the forced march to pursue Greene's withdrawing army. Within a week, the British destroyed their fortifications and evacuated Ninety Six. Marching by night to avoid the heat, British soldiers and a horde of refugee Loyalists left for Charles Town.

The fierce resistance of the Ninety Six garrison can be attributed, in part, to the execution of former Continentals after Hobkirk's Hill. The Tories knew they were doomed if Ninety Six fell. Consequently, they fought on, long after other troops would have surrendered, and won out when relief forces reached them from the coast.

Greene won a strategic victory by besieging Ninety Six. As he did after Hobkirk's Hill, Rawdon destroyed the fortifications and marched toward the coast. This trek was accompanied by many Loyalist families who saw their future go up in the same smoke that consumed Ninety Six. Three of the four key posts on the British defensive screen, Ninety Six, Augusta, and Camden, were now under American control. Only Georgetown remained in British hands and it was evacuated after several attacks.

## Eutaw Springs

Greene marched his army to the High Hills of the Santee near modern-day Columbia to recuperate from their endeavors and train militia sent from the Carolinas, including North Carolina men punished for fleeing at Guilford Courthouse. Reinforcements came in,

> The Tories knew they were doomed if Ninety Six fell. Consequently, they fought on, long after other troops would have surrendered, and won out when relief forces reached them from the coast.

# The Swamp Fox

Francis Marion (1732-1795) is a legendary figure of the Revolutionary War. Known to countless students as the "Swamp Fox," he plagued British and Loyalist forces during their occupation of South Carolina. He first served during the French and Indian War and participated in the attack on Echoe as a lieutenant during 1761.

In the Revolution, Marion was commissioned as captain in the Second South Carolina when the regiment was raised during June 1775. In February 1776, he was promoted to major, transferred to the newly raised Second Regiment of Riflemen and fought at Fort Sullivan during the June 1776 British attack. When the South Carolina Line was placed on the Continental establishment, Marion was promoted to lieutenant colonel of the Second Regiment and led it in the attack on Savannah. Before the British attacked Charleston in spring 1780, Marion was a member of the garrison. He was injured in a fall and evacuated before the city fell May 12, 1780.

After the British occupation was well underway, Marion, who had not signed a parole, began minor raids on the British and released 150 prisoners taken at Camden. It was about this time that Colonel Otho Holland Williams of the Maryland Line noted that Marion's troops "did

MARION AND HIS IRREGULARS MARCH THROUGH A SOUTH CAROLINA SWAMP.

(NPS)

not exceed twenty men and boys, some white, some black, and all mounted, but most of them miserably equipped..."

During fall 1780 and throughout 1781, Marion conducted hit and run raids against British outposts and small marching units.

When Greene returned with Continental troops, Marion cooperated closely with the Southern Army and was often paired with detachments including Lee's Legion to attack posts such as Fort Watson and Georgetown.

Marion earned his "Swamp Fox" sobri-

quet when he successfully eluded Tarleton, who had been sent to capture him, during a November 1780 chase. Marion escaped because he knew the swamps, islands and river system west of Georgetown and Tarleton did not. Operating from his bases at Port Ferry and Snow Island, Marion attacked when conditions favored his operations and withdrew when pressed.

After over a year of raiding and striking at small posts, Marion found himself again in Continental service as he commanded the North and South Carolina militia at Eutaw Springs. Marion's troops were in the first line and performed admirably, firing until their ammunition was gone, then withdrawing under control. The defeat by the Americans cost the British dearly and Marion played an important role.

As the war wound down, Marion took a seat in the South Carolina legislature and was later given their thanks on February 26, 1783 "for his eminent and conspicuous services to his country."

GENERAL FRANCIS MARION OFFERS FOOD TO A BRITISH PRISONER.

(COURTESY ANNE S.K. BROWN MILITARY COLLECTION, BROWN UNIVERSITY)

especially North Carolina Continentals. These unfortunate soldiers had served as militia at Guilford Courthouse. After commanders called their performance dismal, they were forcibly enlisted for a much longer term, drilled intensively and sent to Greene who drilled them even more. In early September, they all marched against British troops camped along the Santee River. The early morning march surprised and captured perhaps 300 British soldiers digging sweet potatoes in a field a short distance from their main encampment at Eutaw Springs.

Greene's army then moved forward in two separate lines. In the front line were four small militia battalions from South and North Carolina under Francis Marion. In the second line were three Continental brigades, one from Maryland on the left under Colonel Otho Holland Williams, the Virginians in the center under Lieutenant Colonel Richard Campbell, and North Carolinians on the right under General Jethro Sumner.

As Greene's army advanced, artillery fire grew more intense but the infantry on both sides stood fast and slugged it out. Two regiments, the 63rd and 64th, covered the British left, in the middle were Cruger's Loyalists from Ninety Six and on the right was the 3rd Regiment, the Buffs. All Crown forces in this engagement were battle hardened veterans. So were most of their opponents.

The American militia slammed into the British line. Fairly well drilled after weeks in camp, the Carolinians fought obstinately. After several volleys, when some militia began to fall back, the British left charged forward. They were counter attacked by Sumner's Continentals who went forward with a rush, aided by Lieutenant Colonel Henry "Light Horse Harry" Lee's dragoons.

The Continentals from Virginia and Maryland replaced other front line units as ammunition ran low. The British began to retreat. At this point, the battle might have been won except for chance. British Major John Majoribanks put his men into a thicket. When William Washington tried to drive them out, he wheeled left in front of the brush. Washington and all

The Continentals from Virginia and Maryland replaced other front lines as ammunition ran low. The British began to retreat. At this point, the battle might have been won except for chance.

but two of his officers were shot down in a British volley. Washington was taken prisoner along with many men. Colonel Alexander Stewart, the British commander, also sent men into the plantation house. Protected by the brick walls, British soldiers fired on passing Americans, diverting both Continentals and militia, and forcing them to engage. Finally, Maryland Continentals, admittedly "thirsty, naked, and fatigued," plundered the camp, especially officer tents in which there was liquor. The Continentals who had remained steady for so long fell behind, leaving their officers to go it virtually alone. One officer who did was John Eager Howard, a hero of Cowpens and Guilford, who was badly wounded. Adding to the confusion, Stewart's men sallied from the house, recapturing artillery taken earlier.

As he had before, Greene opted to withdraw. He broke off the engagement and returned to the High Hills camp. A day later, the British retired to Charles Town. They never came out in force again. After they evacuated Wilmington, North Carolina, the British were confined to Charles Town and Savannah. The Americans constantly nipped at the outer defensive posts, capturing them one by one, steadily decreasing the land holdings and depleting the garrison until the British evacuated the two towns in 1782.

The Americans, including Colonel Washington's command and Colonel Henderson's, moved down to the Eutaw Springs, and the battle there ensued, as well as the fight at the potato patch, two or three miles from the springs. This applicant was in the rear of Washington's troops in the heat of said battle. The British, after giving way, rallied at the brick house and planted some fieldpieces. Washington attacked these pieces, supported by some of Lee's footmen. Washington jumped his horse into the midst of the enemy and was suddenly taken prisoner. A British soldier appearing to be in the posture of attempting to stab Colonel Washington, one of his men rushed forward and cut him down at one blow. Washington being a prisoner, and his men mingled in confusion with the enemy, and not knowing what else to do, this applicant with about twenty-five retreated and left the field. Afterwards they were joined by five of Washington's other soldiers, stating that they only escaped out of a great many who attempted to charge through the enemy's lines, they having succeeded by flight after penetrating through.

— John Chaney, Private, South Carolina Militia

*The Revolution Remembered*, University of Chicago Press, Chicago.

## THE WAR OF POSTS

Throughout the late spring and summer of 1781 while the main armies maneuvered against each other, the partisans went after the widely separated British posts. Initially, when Nathanael Greene returned to South Carolina in April 1781, 8,000 British soldiers under Francis Rawdon were dispersed throughout the state in small garrisons backed up by a field force stationed at Camden. Both sides knew these posts were vulnerable if enough force were brought against them. Greene's strategy was to eradicate the posts and interrupt the British supply system while keeping the Continental Army together as a threat to

Rawdon's army. The British concentrated on destroying Greene's army. Tactically successful on the battlefield, Rawdon's victories produced no gains.

Once back in South Carolina, Greene authorized local leaders, especially Francis Marion, Andrew Pickens, and Thomas Sumter, to attack and sent Henry "Light Horse Harry" Lee and his legion as reinforcements to Francis Marion. Others received weaponry and ammunition. Greene's strategy envisioned partisan leadership coordinating assaults to disrupt the British posts while he moved against stronger points and forced Rawdon to maneuver against the Continental Army.

In short order, British garrisons were attacked. One of the first to fall was Fort Watson where Marion and Lee pinned down the garrison, built a log tower, and shot up the defenders. Fort Watson surrendered on April 23 and some of its garrison, former Continentals, were sent immediately to the main army for courtmartial. Orangeburg surrendered to Sumter on May 11; the next day, Fort Motte was taken by Marion and Lee. On May 15, Lee took Fort Granby and Marion temporarily occupied Georgetown a week later. The raiding went on.

Lee, now assigned to work with Pickens, arrived at Augusta, Georgia, in time to aid in capturing outlying forts and then the main garrison. The British commander, Colonel Thomas Brown, a notorious Tory accused of murder, was fortunate Lee prevented his murder, as one impris-

oned Tory Colonel, Benjamin Grierson was shot by a Patriot assassin. As Lee noted, backcountry warfare exemplified the utmost in barbarity.

Following the surrender of Augusta, Lee and Pickens marched to aid Greene at Ninety Six. The siege at Ninety Six was cut short by the impending arrival of British reinforcements. Unable to carry the fortifications by storm, Greene moved northeast, evading Rawdon's relief force and eventu-

ally taking position in the High Hills from where most American units would march to Eutaw Springs in September.

After Ninety Six, partisans went after the remaining British outposts with a vengeance. In retaliation, Tories under William Cunningham embarked on the "Bloody Campaign." More bloodshed resulted but to little strategic effect.

## THE VIRGINIA CAMPAIGN AND YORKTOWN

During the war, British vessels raided the Chesapeake and its tributaries. These raids were more of a nuisance but they constantly drained the tidewater's resources as ships were captured, burned and scuttled. Virginia built more vessels, especially rowing galleys to protect the coastline. These provided good service, especially when engaged with similar Loyalist boats, but if faced by Royal navy warships and their launches, the galleys usually retired. As with the army, no pay, bad food and little clothing, contributed to a shortage of manpower. The poor funding affected vessels as well.

In October 1780, the British entered the bay in force. Since the Chesapeake was the major thoroughfare for supplies moving south, Clinton felt blocking the bay could materially aid Cornwallis' subjugation of the southern colonies. The British patrolled the Chesapeake until the end of August 1781. Virginia's situation was desperate

BRITISH COMMANDER-IN-CHIEF SIR HENRY CLINTON

(NPS)

BENEDICT ARNOLD

(LC)

because many Virginia Continentals were taken at Charles Town, and new recruits and militia were serving in North Carolina.

In late December 1780, a British force commanded by Brigadier General Benedict Arnold, an American hero turned traitor, led a thrust into Virginia. At the first favorable wind, Arnold went up the James River, hit Richmond and destroyed storehouses full of supplies badly needed by Greene's army. Before effective resistance could be raised, Arnold withdrew down the James and began interfering with shipping.

Washington and Rochambeau sent the Marquis de Lafayette to Virginia to capture the traitor, but the defeat by the British of a French naval force prevented Lafayette's troops in Annapolis, Maryland, from joining him in Virginia. In mid-March, small British and French squadrons fought off the Virginia Capes. The French navy was unable to cooperate with Lafayette because the British retained control of the

48

# French Allies

*"The generous proffs which his most Christian Majesty [King Louis XVI] has given of his attachment to the Cause of America must force conviction on the minds of the most deceived among the Enemy: relatively to the decisive good consequences of the Alliance and inspire every citizen of these States with sentiments of the most unalterable Gratitude."*
— General George Washington, October 20, 1781.

In the French and Indian War (1756-1763), George Washington, commanding Virginia militia troops, had fought alongside British regulars against the French in western Pennsylvania. That war ended a British victory with France ceding most of her holdings in the New World to Great Britain.

When the American Revolutionary War began, France viewed the conflict as a possible opportunity to weaken the British Empire and open American trade markets. However, until the Americans could demonstrate their ability to break free from Great Britain, France limited her assistance to the United States to money and military supplies. After the American capture of a British army at Saratoga, New York in October 1777, France was ready to formalize her support.

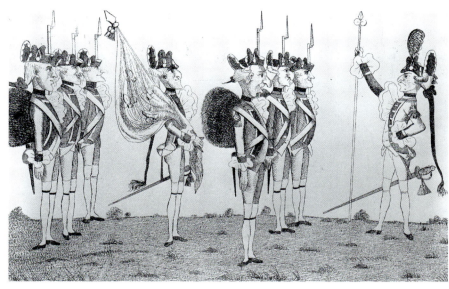

THIS 18TH-CENTURY ENGLISH CARTOON DEPICTS FRENCH GENERAL ROCHAMBEAU REVIEWING THE FRENCH TROOPS.

(LC)

With the signing of the French Alliance in 1778, George Washington found his former enemy now his greatest foreign friend.

France was quick to dispatch a naval battle fleet under Comte d'Estaing to the United States. Unfortunately d'Estaing was unsuccessful against the British and returned to France in 1780, where he, along with the Marquis de Lafayette (who had joined the Continental Army in 1772), helped persuade King Louis XVI to provide further support to their struggling ally.

In the summer of 1780, Comte de Rochambeau arrived in Rhode Island with over 5,000 troops and the following year, another French fleet, with 28 ships-of-the-line (battleships), commanded by Comte de Grasse was dispatched from the Caribbean. The assistance of Rochambeau, his troops, and de Grasse's fleet extensively contributed to Washington's victory at the Siege of Yorktown in 1781.

After Yorktown, the French continued their war with the British, while the United States and Great Britain agreed to provisional peace terms. The United States however, as a condition of the 1778 alliance with France, could not sign a formal treaty with Great Britain until France and Great Britain had reached a similar agreement ending their war. In 1783, almost two years after the victory at Yorktown, Great Britain signed multiple treaties of Paris, ending her conflict with France and conceding independence of her 13 American colonies.

Early in the war American diplomats sought French officers who could provide the experience and military expertise the Continental Army was lacking. In 1777, Lieutenant-Colonel Louis Duportail was one of four French military engineers sent to the United States. Congress designated him Chief of Engineers, with the rank of brigadier general. In May 1780 he was captured with American forces at Charleston, South Carolina. He was exchanged and rejoined the Continental Army and served as Washington's chief engineer at the Siege of Yorktown. His services at this classically conducted European style siege were invaluable and for his work he was promoted to major general. In 1783 he returned to France, but several years later, difficulties during the French Revolution forced him to flee to the United States. In 1802 he was sailing to France when he died at sea.
— Diane Depew, Colonial NHP

MARIE JOSEPH PAUL YVES ROCH GILBERT DU MOTIER, MARQUIS DE LAFAYETTE

(LC)

bay. The French squadron returned to Newport, Rhode Island. Lafayette, without naval support, rejoined his troops in Annapolis.

With firm control of the Chesapeake Bay, General Clinton sent 2,000 additional troops, commanded by Major General William Phillips to Virginia. Phillips took command over Arnold and his forces. In April, the British went to Petersburg. They then destroyed or captured James River shipping below Richmond.

Cornwallis entered Virginia in mid-May. As he said in a letter to Clinton, "I mean to possess the country sufficiently to overturn the Rebel government." Taking command of all British forces in Virginia because Phillips had recently died, Cornwallis moved to Petersburg and then beyond Richmond. Tarleton's British Legion raided toward the Blue Ridge, snatched some Virginia legislators, and nearly caught Governor Thomas Jefferson and others who fled just ahead of the

British cavalry. Lafayette's forces, often out-numbered four to one, sparred with the raiders but could not force them away. Baron Von Steuben, the drillmaster of the Continental Army, tried to coordinate supplies for both Greene's Army and Lafayette's Continentals.

In June, Clinton instructed Cornwallis to "take a defensive station, in any healthy situation you choose (be it at Williamsburg or Yorktown)." There Cornwallis was to prepare some of his army for transfer to New York City, where Clinton was faced with a possible combined attack by General Washington and his French ally, the Comte de Rochambeau. In the summer of 1780, Rochambeau, along with 5,500 French soldiers, had sailed into Newport, Rhode Island, prepared to offer valuable assistance to the Continental Army.

Cornwallis moved to Williamsburg and in early July, planned to move his army across the James River at Jamestown, then proceed along the south side of the river to Portsmouth. Lafayette, who had shadowed Cornwallis' movements, perceived an opportunity to attack a portion of the British army as it was astride the James River. Brigadier General Anthony Wayne and 800 Continental troops had recently reinforced Lafayette and with Virginia militia joining his ranks, Lafayette lessened his numerical disadvantage to two to one. On July 6, Lafayette saw his opportunity to attack and sent Wayne and his brigade to reconnoiter the British position and verify that only a small portion of the British army remained north of the James River. Near Green Spring Plantation, Wayne encountered British pickets. Surprised by the resolve of the British, Lafayette moved to get a better view of the British positions and discovered that Wayne was entering a British trap. The British had not moved most of their army across the river, but had deceived Lafayette that they had done the opposite. By the time Lafayette gave the news of the British strength to Wayne, his

GENERAL ANTHONY WAYNE

(HISTORICAL SOCIETY OF PENNSYLVANIA)

The American riflemen insulted the outposts, whilst a body of continentals advanced towards the morass: The British cavalry supported the pickets on the left, in order to contain the enemy within the woods, and to prevent their viewing the main army: Earl Cornwallis ... ordered the battalions and regiments to remain quiet in their cap, where they were concealed ... the Marqis de la Fayette had passed the morass on the left, with about six hundred militia, nine hundred continentals, and some cannon; bodies of riflemen attacked the other pickets ... Upon the first cannon shot from the enemy, the British army formed and advanced ...

Lieutenant-colonel Dundas's Brigade, composed of the 43d, 76th, and 80th regiments, with two six-pounders, under Captain Fage, sustained the weight of the enemy's attack. The conflict in this quarter was severe and well contested. The artillery and infantry of each army, in presence of their respective generals, were for some minutes warmly engaged not fifty yards asunder. The other part of the line ... met with little or no resistance, being opposed only by small parties of militia ... on the left of the Briitsh, the action was for some time gallantly maintained by the continental infantry, under General Wayne, against the 76th, 80th, and part of the 43d. The legion cavalry formed a second line behind the 80th, and the light companies, under Captain Champagne, dismounted to reinforce the 76th. The affair was not ended before dark, when the enemy abandoned their cannon, and repassed the swamp in confusion.

—Banastre Tarleton, Lieutenant Colonel, British Legion

*A History of the Campaigns of 1780 and 1781 in the Southern Provinces of North America,* T. Cadell, London.

brigade was already heavily engaged. A withdrawal so close to the enemy did not seem feasible, so Lafayette ordered up reinforcements. With additional troops, Wayne ordered an assault, which temporarily halted the British advance and enabled the Americans to withdraw. Estimated Patriot battle losses in the Battle of Green

> A withdrawal so close to the enemy did not seem feasible, so Lafayette ordered up reinforcements. With additional troops, Wayne ordered an assault, which temporarily halted the British advance and enabled the Americans to withdraw.

**In the meantime, Washington's plans to attack Clinton in New York City were falling apart. When Washington and Comte de Rochambeau met to discuss mutual operations, the French commander suggested attacking Cornwallis in Virginia.**

Spring, the largest infantry engagement in Virginia during the war, were 28 killed, 99 wounded and 12 missing. Combined losses for the British numbered around 75.

Cornwallis moved on, and in early August occupied the port of Yorktown on the York River as well as Gloucester Point across the river. Yorktown, with its docks, wharves, and deep water access to the Chesapeake Bay, seemed a good place to establish a naval base. Slaves, promised freedom in exchange for assisting the British, began building fortifications at both Gloucester Point and Yorktown, as Cornwallis prepared for the arrival of the British navy.

In the meantime, Washington's plans to attack Clinton in New York City were falling apart. When Washington and Comte de Rochambeau met to discuss mutual operations, the French commander suggested attacking Cornwallis in Virginia. In mid-August, Washington learned a French battle fleet with 28 battleships and 3,000 troops was sailing for the Chesapeake under Comte Francois-Joseph-Paul de Grasse and was not coming to support his operations in New York. Seizing the

opportunity to go after Cornwallis, the allies shifted their armies around New York, implying they would attack Staten Island. Instead, the allies suddenly marched south, boarded transports at the head of the Chesapeake Bay and sailed to Virginia. Siege equipment was shipped from Newport, Rhode Island, in a small French battle fleet, the same fleet that had transported Rochambeau's army to America the previous year.

A key naval engagement was about to take place. Its outcome would determine, as Washington's troops were marching south, whether upon their arrival in Virginia an attack against Cornwallis would be worth attempting.

In the West Indies, de Grasse sent his fleet northward, under the eye of Britain's Admiral George Rodney. Rodney dispatched Admiral Samuel Hood to locate the French fleet. Hood checked the mouth of the Chesapeake on August 25, saw no French ships and continued sailing north for New York City. On August 31, de Grasse, who had taken a longer and more circuitous route, sailed into the Chesapeake. Even then, the British had a chance. The same day the French fleet reached the Chesapeake, British Admiral Thomas Graves, with 19 battleships left New York City, moving south in search of de Grasse.

On September 5, the British fleet approached the entrance to the Chesapeake, surprising the French ships at anchor with some of their sailors on shore. Admiral Graves had the advantage of wind and tide but de Grasse moved 24 of his battleships to engage the British. Both fleets maneuvered in parallel battle lines, seeking advantage. At 4:00 P.M., fighting began as the British turned toward the French. Over the next two hours, the lead-

ADMIRAL JOSEPH-PAUL
DE GRASSE

(NA)

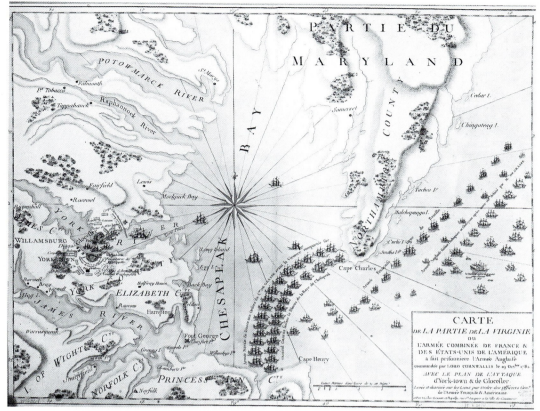

THIS 1781 MAP SHOWS
ADMIRAL DE GRASSE'S
FRENCH FLEET IN
CHESAPEAKE BAY.

(LC)

ing elements battered each other. The two fleets spent the night in close proximity, sailing in battle formation ready to renew the fighting. The fleets did not engage again. On September 9, the British fleet changed course for New York and the French returned to the Chesapeake Bay, joining the French ships that had recently arrived from Newport, Rhode Island, carrying siege artillery.

Washington and Rochambeau reached Williamsburg, Virginia, on September 14 and linked up with Lafayette. The French and American armies from the north began arriving September 21. On September 28, the Americans and French troops, some 17,000 men, marched against Yorktown and Cornwallis.

Later that day, the allied troops encountered the British outposts around Yorktown. Small, scattered skirmishing took place as George Washington and Rochambeau established the armies'

camps and prepared for a formal siege. On October 6, the allies constructed their first siege line, 1,000 yards from the main British defenses. Three days later, the allied siege guns opened fire from the first siege line.

On October 11, the allies started a second siege line within 400 yards of the British. Positioned within the eventual path of the second siege line were two British forward positions, small earthen forts, Redoubts 9 and 10 that protected the British left flank. On the night of October 14, Redoubt 9 was stormed by 400 French regulars, while 400 American Light Infantry under Lieutenant Colonel Alexander Hamilton assaulted Redoubt 10. Within 30 minutes both redoubts were captured and the following day, the allies completed their second siege line. Trapped within point blank artillery range, and being bombarded night and day, Cornwallis attempted an overland escape. If he

# Yorktown

The English and the other troops were more heavily bombed and lost many men. This continued day and night. Our batteries were shot to pieces and demolished. We had to repair them during the night, which caused us to lose many troops engaged in the work. We hoped each day to see our main army but it did not come.... During the night a bomb hit our powder magazine, blew it up, and some English artillerymen were killed. Our battery was shot up so badly that we could use only one cannon. We had cannons enough but no gun carriages for them, no powder, no cannonballs remained, and only a few English artillerymen were still alive. — Sergeant Koch, Vontruembach Hessian Regiment

*Enemy Views: The American Revolutionary War as Recorded by the Hessian Participants,* Heritage Books, Bowie, Maryland; 1996.

I saw several officers fixing bayonets on long staves. I then concluded we were about to make a general assault upon the enemy's works, but before dark I was informed of the whole plan, which was to storm the redoubts, the one by the Americans, the other by the French. The Sappers and Miners were furnished with axes and were to proceed in front and cut a passage for the troops through the abatis which are composed of the tops of trees, the small branches cut off with a slanting stroke which renders them as sharp as spikes. ... At dark the detachment ... advanced beyond the trenches and lay down ... Our watchword was "Rochambeau," the commander of the French ... being pronounced *Ro-sham-bow*, it sounded, when pronounced quick, like *ruch-on-boys*. ... I could not pass at the entrance we had made, it was so crowded. I therefore forced a passage at a place where I saw our shot had cut away some of the abatis; ... a man at my side received a ball in his head and fell under my feet, crying out bitterly. ... the enemy threw hand grenades (small shells) ... they were so thick that I at first thought them cartridge papers on fire, but was soon undeceived by their cracking. — Joseph Plumb Martin, Sergeant, Continental Corps of Sappers and Miners

*Private Yankee Doodle — Being a Narrative of some of the Adventures, Dangers and Sufferings of a Revolutionary Soldier,* Eastern Acorn Press; 1979.

On this day ... I went for the last time on the engineer watch. At twelve o'clock noon all watches and posts were cancelled. Only a regimental watch of one sergeant with twelve men remained on duty ... The French and Americans immediately occupied our works ... We were, on one side, happy that finally this siege was ended ... because we always believed we would be taken by storm. If it had continued only a few more days, it would really have resulted in a major attack. ... during this siege the enemy had thrown more than eight thousand bombs... Under the terms of the capitulation ... Cornwallis was allowed two safe ships, that is, ships that could not be searched and were allowed free, unhindered passage to New York; and on those he was allowed to send out many members of the .... loyalists ... as well as many deserters who had gone over to the English from the French and Americans. ... General Cornwallis and Lieutenant Colonel Tarleton also went aboard.
— Johann Conrad Dohla, Private, Ansbach-Bayreuth Hessians

*A Hessian Diary of the American Revolution by Johann Conrad Dohla,* University of Oklahoma Press, Norman, Oklahoma; 1990.

WASHINGTON FIRING THE FIRST AMERICAN GUN AT YORKTOWN.

(LC)

could move his army across the river to Gloucester Point, it might be possible to break through the American and French lines there and retreat northward, possibly as far as New York City. Around midnight of October 16, about 1,000 British troops had made it across the river when a sudden storm prevented further crossings. By sunrise the attempt was abandoned.

On October 17, the allied bombardment was intense, with 60-70 allied siege cannon pounding the British. With no expectation that a British relief fleet and reinforcements would reach him soon, Cornwallis requested a cease fire to negotiate surrender terms. On October 18, the Articles of Capitulation were agreed upon and the following day, October 19, the British marched out of their defenses to formally surrender. In response for denying full "honors of war" to the Americans at Charles Town, the British had been granted similar terms. During the surrender ceremony, the British military musicians were not allowed to play American or French tunes, which was considered a professional salute to the victor and their regimental flags were kept cased. Cornwallis, pleading

illness, had his second-in-command, General Charles O'Hara, formally surrender the army. O'Hara tried to surrender Cornwallis's sword, first to Rochambeau; who directed him to Washington and then Washington motioned him to surrender to the American second-in-command, Benjamin Lincoln. Lincoln, the general who had been denied the honors of war after his gallant defense of Charles Town, accepted the sword from O'Hara.

## EPILOGUE

After Eutaw Springs and Yorktown, the war was not officially over, but the major fighting had ended. The British military could not recover from the loss of Cornwallis's army. As diplomats began negotiating for a formal end to the war, the final efforts to completely free the southern coast dragged on. Pennsylvania, Delaware and Maryland Continentals went south from Yorktown and joined Greene's army. When they finally arrived, many long-suffering Southern army veterans were granted furloughs and went home.

Greene moved southeast of Charles Town and continued harassing the British while protecting South Carolina legislative meetings. One spoiling attack on a rowing galley cost the life of the very popular John Laurens, a South Carolina Light Infantryman who had served on Washington's staff. Anthony Wayne took the Pennsylvanians and the Light Infantry into Georgia where they blockaded Savannah, defeated a British and Indian raiding party, and effectively besieged the town. In July 1782, the British finally evacuated Savannah. Charles Town followed later in the year. In September 1783, the British formally signed the Treaty of Paris, recognizing the independence of the United States of America.

---

# GLORIOUS NEWS.

### PROVIDĔCE, October 25, 1781.

#### Three o'Clock, P. M.

THIS MOMENT an EXPRESS arrived at his Honour the Deputy-Governor's, from Col. Christopher Olney, Commandant on Rhode-Island, announcing the important Intelligence of the Surrender of Lord Cornwallis and his Army, an Account of which was printed This Morning at Newport, and is as follows, viz.

#### Newport, October 25, 1781.

YESTERDAY afternoon arrived in this Harbour Capt. Lovett, of the Schooner Adventure, from York-River, in Chesapeak-Bay (which he left the 20th Instant) and brought us the glorious News of the Surrender of Lord CORNWALLIS and his Army Prisoners of War to the allied Army, under the Command of our illustrious General, and the French Fleet, under the Command of his Excellency the Count de GRASSE.

A Cessation of Arms took Place on Thursday the 18th Instant, in Consequence of Proposals from Lord Cornwallis for a Capitulation. His Lordship proposed a Cessation of Twenty-four Hours, but Two only were granted by His Excellency General WASHINGTON. The Articles were completed the same Day, and the next Day the allied Army took Possession of York-Town.

By this glorious Conquest, NINE THOUSAND of the Enemy, including Seamen, fell into our Hands, with an immense Quantity of Warlike Stores, a forty Gun Ship, a Frigate, an armed Vessel, and about One Hundred Sail of Transports.

THE "GLORIOUS NEWS" OF THE SURRENDER OF CORNWALLIS

(LC)

THIS 1782 PRINT IS TITLED *AMERICA TRIUMPHANT AND BRITANNIA IN DISTRESS.*

(LC)